How to Get Into Ivy League College

How to Nudge Your Cub Into a Quality College

(A Quick Guide to Help You Getting Into Your Dream University)

Patrick Hunt

Published By **Regina Loviusher**

Patrick Hunt

All Rights Reserved

How to Get Into Ivy League College: How to Nudge Your Cub Into a Quality College (A Quick Guide to Help You Getting Into Your Dream University)

ISBN 978-1-77485-793-9

No part of this guidebook shall be reproduced in any form without permission in writing from the publisher except in the case of brief quotations embodied in critical articles or reviews.

Legal & Disclaimer

The information contained in this ebook is not designed to replace or take the place of any form of medicine or professional medical advice. The information in this ebook has been provided for educational & entertainment purposes only.

The information contained in this book has been compiled from sources deemed reliable, and it is accurate to the best of the Author's knowledge; however, the Author cannot guarantee its accuracy and validity and cannot be held liable for any errors or omissions. Changes are periodically made to this book. You must consult your doctor or get professional medical advice before using any of the suggested remedies, techniques, or information in this book.

Upon using the information contained in this book, you agree to hold harmless the Author from and against any damages, costs, and expenses, including any legal fees potentially resulting from the application of any of the information provided by this guide. This disclaimer applies to any damages or injury caused by the use and application, whether directly or indirectly, of any advice or information presented, whether for breach of contract, tort, negligence, personal injury, criminal intent, or under any other cause of action.

You agree to accept all risks of using the information presented inside this book. You need to consult a professional medical practitioner in order to ensure you are both able and healthy enough to participate in this program.

Table Of Contents

Chapter 1: Who Is The Right Ivy League School For?................................. 1

Chapter 2: After A Week....................... 11

Chapter 3: Be Different........................ 19

Chapter 4: How To Stay Motivated 26

Chapter 5: How To Stand Out To The Ivy League With The Achieve System 36

Chapter 6: Step 1 Of Achieve– Aim For As In Advanced Classes............................. 42

Chapter 7: Step 2 Of Achieve - Conduct An Activity Audit 67

Chapter 8: Step 3 Of Achieve - Help Your Teacher Help You 80

Chapter 9: Step 4 Of Achieve - Ignite Your Interests 92

Chapter 10: Step 5 Of Achieve............ 116

Chapter 11: Step 6 Of Achieve - Validate Your Credibility 139

Chapter 1: Who Is The Right Ivy League School For?

What do you think of when you think about Ivy League? Are you thinking about Gilmore Girls or ivory towers? It's full of smart, wealthy, preppy students. Because I didn't know many people who went top schools, that's how it felt to me.

I attended a Chinese Bible Study Group when I was 10 years old. I had the opportunity to talk to Lili, a neighbor's daughter. She grumbled as she walked up to the other children. "Everyone at Harvard is so smarter than I am."

Even though I was in elementary school, I thought she would feel dumb if she did. It's possible you feel the same. Maybe you are wondering if you'd do well even if your dream Ivy League is achieved. Are you able to keep up with the pace?

This is because, even though I was from a public school with a decent AP program, it didn't compare to top prep schools with the best tutors. I was afraid I would be outclassed.

Do you feel dumb?

Both yes and no. It is important to remember that you will be going to school alongside the brightest and best students from around the globe. Although you may have been at the top of your class before, now you will be with all the students. Focusing on one skill, such as your physics skills, can make you feel stupid.

If you can see that everyone is a mix of strengths and weaknesses, and that each person is unique, then you won't feel stupid. One of my classmates was an example. He had perfect pitch, was a musician genius, but struggled with procrastination. Teachers had to remind him three times a day to submit assignments. Another of my classmates was the most articulate and clear writer I had ever seen. However, he struggled with basic math.

We are all different.

Focus on your strengths, and find people to complement them. My strength is in networking and connecting people so I used that strength to find people I believed would be great friends. Two of my closest friends shared the same interests in classical music and physics as I did in German language. They were finishing each others sentences by the end of the meeting!

One of my Harvard classmates told me that it was hard to get into Harvard, but not difficult to graduate. I was in shock from high school, and I was star-struck to have been accepted at Harvard. But I eventually realized that this quote was true. You have weekly office hours with your teachers' assistants. Peer tutors are available. There were also tutoring centers that provided free writing and math tutoring almost every day. Harvard and other schools are committed to your success after you have been admitted.

My Calculus B/C class presented me with open-ended homework. I was unable to complete it. It was easier for me to take the course in highschool. High school teachers would give similar examples and lecture. While you would learn the basics, college will give you four questions for homework. Instead of 30 questions, I was given four difficult, theoretical questions to complete my homework. I reached out to my classmates for help and attended the math question center nearly every day. I persevered and was able to complete the class. I also made friends.

You could show your gratitude and courage by going to your professor's office. After the meeting, you could also use your gratitude to send them an email thanking them. It will be easier to ask for assistance later if you have built a friendship. You can succeed at the Ivy League if you ask for help when in trouble. It is okay to struggle with a topic; everyone can benefit from some assistance in certain classes.

Is everyone at Ivies pretentious?

I was not the only one who thought Ivy League was for geniuses. I also believed that I would be surrounded with preppy children. I wanted to make an impression and fit in so I did some research on the Ivy League and created a list of all the sweaters and jeans I needed.

I couldn't afford to buy Ralph Lauren or Citizen For Humanity jeans at full price so I stopped by Goodwill in a better neighborhood. I was able find cashmere sweaters at 9 dollars and designer jeans for 15 bucks. These deals are so rare.

Harvard was my first choice because I had a lot of prepped clothes. I can vividly recall walking into the freshman dining room, which looked like something out of Harry Potter. I realized that I was wrong. I was the most preppy, overdressed person there. Students wore t-shirts, nondescript jeans and t-shirts. Some students looked as though they just got out of bed in sweatshirts and sweatpants. From a California public school where many girls wore make-up, and most guys shaved their heads, it was shocking to see people without makeup and men who had grown their beards in strange, month-based manliness challenges.

I was shocked to learn that Ivy League students are not voted "best dressed" and "most chic" in senior yearbooks. It was all a myth that I had imagined a preppy style. I was the Harvard student who looked the most stylish because of my misguided preparation.

Are all the Ivies wealthy?

Although it might seem that the Ivy League is reserved for wealthy kids, the truth is quite different. They do a lot of work to attract students with low incomes and provide the best financial aid for middle-class families.

Harvard has a median parent contribution of only $1,050. $12,000 since 55% students receive financial aid. [1] The cost of your financial aid is calculated based on your family income. Search Harvard's net price calculator for an estimate. Many colleges offer a similar calculator for financial aid on their websites.

Although the price tag for an Ivy League education may seem high, it is possible to afford the real cost. If you didn't receive any aid to Yale in 2021 you would pay $81,000 annually. [2] Although some families are able to afford this sticker price, it is still more than the average American makes in a year. Yale and other elite schools offer generous financial aid awards to help families. You would pay approximately $15,000 per year if your family's income was $100,000 to $150,000 in 2021. Only 19% of the sticker cost! It would drop from there.

International students may also be eligible for financial aid from some schools of the Ivy League. Columbia University, for example, offered 299 international students an annual financial award of $71,069 and Harvard, 605 international students, an average financial award at $66,805. [4] However, not all universities are able to afford to be as generous. Check out the financial aid website of your dream college to find out how much you could be expected to receive.

The Ivy League is not just for the wealthy. Many top schools offer great financial benefits to students of lower and middle income, regardless of whether they are from abroad.

The Ivy League is not for everyone

The Ivy League is still an option for you, even if your family isn't wealthy, preppy or genius. However, it could be difficult for you if your academic skills are poor.

All of us have strong and weak subjects. Honors/AP/IB classes will challenge you. However, if you find these classes too difficult, the Ivy League may not be the right fit for you. That's fine. There are many great colleges.

You will be challenged in many classes by the Ivy League, and you'll need help. This isn't high school. The teacher only has 30 students in each class, so they have the time and resources to help you with missing assignments. They can also chat with you if your work isn't getting through. Many intro classes are packed with hundreds of students so it's important to be proactive and ask for help if you have any questions. There are many office hours available with teachers' assistants. Your peers can also be great study partners.

The Ivy League is not well-known for its mental health services. It's hard enough to be away from family and friends. Make sure you have a strong mental foundation and spend time with your closest friends and supporters once you get there.

Summary

In this first chapter, you busted the myths and misconceptions about the Ivy League, like that it's only for the rich, the preppy, and the geniuses.

You learned that the sticker price of the Ivy League schools can be misleading, since there's lots of scholarships and financial aid that scales based on your family's income.

At the same time, the Ivy League is not for everyone, and if you struggle to ask for help, you'll have a very tough time without your parents or high school teachers around.

Action Steps

Check out the financial aid websites for the college to which you are applying

Based on your family income, calculate how much you will pay for your projected cost.

Write down 2 strengths

Chapter 2: After A Week

All his rejection letters were returned and he was not invited to interview for the first round. He decided to look into adding a college brand to his resume.

Within one hour, he received an email from the recruiter requesting a first round interview. The job was not for him (since that would have been lying on your resume and could result in you being fired), but he did get an email back from the recruiter. You can get into top schools by changing your university name.

What made the difference?

This story shocked me. Although he ended up in the same tech company that I did, I could clearly see how my path to the job was simpler and more direct.

After graduating college, I entered strategy consulting. This allowed me to help companies expand their business by understanding market trends and how they compare to other competitors. It was easy to land a highly soughtafter consulting job, as many top consulting firms hire on campus at all Ivy Leagues. After 2 years, I made the decision to move to the tech sector. It was easy to get interviews for my first round and eventually land a job in highpaying tech.

Marc Andreessen is a venture capitalist, entrepreneur and author. His podcast A16z explains that employers used personality and IQ tests to screen applicants in the past. However, this became unacceptable socially. Employers wanted a way of screening for intelligence and attention to detail. So they turned to the college name to be a substitute. Employers will consider where you went to college an important factor in assessing your intelligence and ability to work.

My coworker worked for many years as a contractor, without the coveted benefits of paid time off, paid vacations, or healthcare, and with fixed ending dates. Before he could become a full-time employee in a tech company, he had to prove his worth.

Life is easier with an Ivy League degree

Two things are evident. It is possible to get a job in tech, even if your school wasn't a top one. However, the process may take longer and be more difficult. Brand college names such as the Ivy League can help you pass the initial round of resume screening, and land more opportunities.

I interviewed another student who attended an Ivy League college, then went on to Stanford to complete his PhD program. He also mentioned that credibility is a key factor in getting into graduate school.

The Ivy League offers valuable alumni networks and credibility to your college. Alumni networks are the alumni who have been to the school and can provide unique opportunities for students.

Harvard's alumni network allowed me to land internships at large consumer goods companies, executive recruitment firms, and popular TV shows all while I was still in college. My Harvard classmate founded a company together with another Harvard student. You can either reach out to your network or alumni to offer the opportunity. People are more inclined to help others who are like them. If you attended the same school as them, you'll likely get help.

The Ivy League has more resources

Talking to my friends at UC Berkeley, it was surprising to learn that students had to deal with a lack in funding on a daily basis. Due to the school's size, there was a sink-or-swim mentality. UC Berkeley has been relying on students from other states to help them with their money problems. [5]

Funding should not be a concern for students. The school should ensure that all students are able to focus on their grades as well as getting involved in the college community.

Harvard was a place where I discovered the common refrain "It's difficult to get in but not hard for you to graduate" to be completely true. You just need to ask for it. Every freshman is introduced to tons and tons of people who can help you. Each dormitory has a resident adviser (R.A.). This person lives nearby and offers study breaks with snacks. A peer mentor is an upperclassman who can connect with you and checks in with your room.

Your professors and teaching assistants are available to help you with your academic needs. There's the math resource center that is open every night and is staffed by math tutors and peer tutors who can help with homework. You also have the writing center where you can review drafts of essays or study with a peer tutor who has already achieved an A or better in your class.

You will feel supported

After leaving the track team, one of my classmates lost his motivation and began to procrastinate. He was eventually failing his classes. Harvard helped him to take time off from work to mature, and then return to school to finish his studies.

The best in academia

An Ivy degree will not only help you achieve your career goals but it also allows you to attend one the oldest educational institutions in the United States. Harvard, which was founded in 1636, is the oldest higher education institution in America. [6] Other Ivies were established in the 18th Century.

This is a way to be reminded of great scholars like Ralph Waldo Emerson, who has the philosophy building named in his honor, or William James, the original psychologist, who enrolled at Harvard in 1861. His name now rests on Harvard's psychology building. [7]

In one class of government, I recall that we were discussing what one the most prominent political scholars meant by his writing.

My teacher told me, "You can ask him. He's just down the hall."

It was shocking. It was in this same building that many of the most influential political scholars lived. This is true for both government majors and economics majors.

An Ivy gives you access to the top leaders in the field. You will also be surrounded with a place that has maintained the highest standards of education, pedagogy and knowledge pursuit for centuries!

Summary

In this chapter, you learned some of the reasons it's beneficial to go to an Ivy League school.

Whether it's the abundance of resourc es, financial aid, world class teachers, amazing classmates, or incredible professional network, going to a top school has lifetime benefits that will help you find jobs easier and accelerate your career.

Action Steps

Think about how the Ivy League could benefit you in your career. Do you plan to attend grad school?

Chapter 3: Be Different

This is something we all share: We are great at comparing ourselves with others. We are upset when our peers do more than us. We plan how to make up the difference and become better. Sometimes envy and jealousy can sink deep into our souls and demotivate. It is one thing to compare and imitate. This will make you yet another applicant package that is likely to be rejected by a top school.

But imagine if you stopped more often. You might find things you enjoy and are passionate about. You can stop wasting your time comparing yourself to others and start to chart your own course. You might become a famous comedian or writer. There are endless possibilities. Your possibilities are limitless.

Fitting in is addictive

When you are comfortable, there are no awkward questions. You are loved by others. You are the status quo. There are friends like you who share similar interests and are your same age. It's good to feel connected.

You won't feel accepted if you are different. It can be very frustrating to feel isolated and lonely. Social rejection is painful, so we want to be accepted. Research shows that the brain experiences rejection in a similar way to physical pain. [8]

That pain has been a constant battle for me. I was not a very social high school student and often wondered what it would have been like to be "normal" high-school student.

It was easy to get over it when I reminded myself why I was doing it. Your secret reserve is your "why". It is the fuel that keeps your energy going when you feel exhausted. You must be emotionally charged with your why. If you find it easy to cry, your why should bring you to tears.

It was about making my family's lives better. Growing up in a chaotic home full of violence, fighting and hatred, I was raised. I didn't just want to escape, I also wanted to make a better world for others.

Find your escape

Escape is something that takes your mind off of all worries. It is an activity that will give you energy, but not drain you. It is an activity that makes you feel alive and can make you forget about time.

It is a way to give back to the community, and make the world a better place. It's fine if you don't know one. This is something you can do over time.

It was teaching. It was that moment when a student I was tutoring understood it. It would sometimes be a simple math problem that I had to explain in four different ways until they understood. Teaching public speaking and debate was a passion of mine. These skills give you the ability to speak up, to be heard, to advocate for yourself, and to gain attention.

My chaotic family made it difficult for me to feel like I could speak up. Speech and debate helped fill that gap.

The work never ends

It's a good thing that if you can find your escape, you'll feel less like you are working and more motivated to continue.

You will always be resentful of fitting in. It is easy to be expected to conform to the norm and find it exhausting. It is never easy to be different.

If you do the work, you will stand out

Here is where you need to find your "why". It should be strong enough to keep the fire burning.

Pick a specific person in the group to help you reach your goal of inspiring teens and young adults to find voice. You can imagine your cousin, your sister or someone else. Think about how they will benefit from your activity. They will be able to face bullies with confidence. They will be able to stand up against poor managers. They will feel empowered to pursue their own interests and not those of others.

You can be different in a world where everyone copies each other's moves.

There's no better time than now to get started. You will be more successful at being different and you'll be accepted to top schools. Most importantly, you will be able to move towards being the person that you want to be.

Why does this matter?

You will constantly be bombarded by stories about what others are doing, whether it is on social media, with their parents or gossiping grandmas. It will be tempting to follow the footsteps of your older siblings. If you give in to that temptation, you'll be living other lives than your own. You have the right to live your life, follow your passions, and reach your goals.

These opportunities won't just appear by themselves. They would not be there if they did. Your classmates would take advantage.

These items can be found at thrift stores, or even built by you.

What you really need to do

It is centered around the two-word mentality, Be Different. You can do things that no one else, not just adults, would be able to do. My first job was at the age of 14. My classmates asked me, "Is it possible to get a job at this age?" I replied, "Yes, you can get work permits at 14 or younger in certain fields." It was something I had researched online.

It was actually my unintentional creation of my own internship. My counselor at high school, Mrs. K., heard me mention my passion for Law and referred me to local Law offices that could help with filing documents and assisting lawyers. Boom. Internships paid.

It is important to not listen to other people's opinions. It is important to resist the opinions of your parents.

It is not enough to join clubs because your friends do it. You can take an example of journalism, academic decathlon and honor society. To have a "accomplished" resume, stop doing all the useless activities. Make a decision to be different.

Summary

In this chapter, you learned that comparing yourself to others is not only common but a default that we must break in order to be true to ourselves.

There are countless other students who want to get into the Ivy League, so you have to adopt a mentality of "being different" to make sure the admissions officers remember you.

One way to be different is by going all-in on the activities that inspire you most and resisting other people's opinions. Action Steps

Ask yourself questions such as: What would you do if money wasn't an object? What activities do I participate in that make the most of my strengths? Are there any careers or topics that interest me?

Chapter 4: How To Stay Motivated

Our house was well known by the cops. My family was constantly fighting for money after the 2001 telecom recession. Sometimes it ended in the police knocking at our front door.

"Stop crying, child. I was told by a police officer to be calm like my sister. How could I remain calm in a home that was so financially distressed? They couldn't give me an answer so I focused all my energy on creating a better future for my family.

I knew that I would have a better future if I got into the best college I could. I decided to pursue the Ivies in my quest to escape my chaotic family in California. It was also a high-stakes game. Because my parents couldn't afford college, I had to apply for a full-ride scholarship.

I spent every second of my day strategizing how I could be different to the Ivy League, and not getting distracted by the fighting and divisions in our home. To block out the noise,

I first bought over-the-ear headphones. I then took out the TV and filled in my planner. Then, I was able to access the library at the nearby community college by dual enrollment. This is when you can take college classes while still in high school.

It was a grind

I was able to take almost all of the difficult classes at my school. I also

did internships and held leadership positions.

Every day, my schedule looked this way:

7:45am: Wake up, have a cup of coffee, and get to school

7:30-3pm: attend school

3-6pm: cross-country practice

6-7:30pm: Get home and eat three bowls of rice.

7-8pm: math homework

8-9pm: science homework

9-10pm: English homework

10-11pm: study Spanish

11:15pm: Shower, go to bed with wet hair. Grandma will scold you to dry it.

Because I was not a natural test-taker, I spent over 2 hours a day practicing ACT tests in senior year. It paid off. My score went up from 30 to 34, which is the highest possible score. This is enough to get into top schools. As I was sure I would need to pay for school, I spent hours each day searching for scholarships. Thanks to the Bill and Melinda Gates Foundation, I was able to get a full ride to any college that I chose. [9] For a free bonus video on how to find scholarships, visit www.ivyguides.com/free. You can get through the grind if you have a "why". My "why" was that I wanted to work harder now in order to have a better future and less money struggles than my family. Perhaps your "why" is that you have lost a friend to the disease and want to raise money to help fund research to find a cure. Perhaps your "why" is because you are passionate about animals and believe they deserve better treatment and more rights. Maybe you are inspired by the hard work of your family and want to give them a better quality life.

Your source of motivation

Which do you think is more likely to succeed? Bob, who is only interested in becoming a doctor for the money, or Sally who wants to live a longer and healthier life because her father, who has diabetes, struggles to make ends meet. Which one is more likely to persevere after failing an organic chemistry exam?

You are probably right, Sally. Your secret source of energy is your "why". It is the fuel that keeps your going through all the AP/IB, advancedclass homework. Sally's purpose-driven "whys" may not be the same as others. Premium-grade fuel is what she uses.

Even though you might be stuck in quarantine or not being able to visit your friends, it keeps you going. Even if you don't understand physics or think it's too difficult for you, it keeps you going. Even though others tell you they don't think you can get into Ivy, or that your dreams are too big, it keeps you going. You can.

Perhaps your "why" is about making a better family or developing mentorship for women working in STEM. This is just one reason why we need more women in STEM. [10]

You will be noticed if you put in the effort. Your "why" is crucial. It should be a strong "why", which keeps the fire burning. Pick a specific person in the group you want to target if your mission is to inspire teenagers and young adults to find their voice. You could, for example, host a class on public speaking to 8-graders. It gives Tina confidence and she goes on to become a leader in social justice movements. Maybe you helped your cousin fight bullies, and now you want cyberbullying policies.

Visualize how your activities will benefit those you care about. Visualizing the positive effects of your work will keep you motivated.

You have no better time to discover your "why" than now. You are more likely to get admitted to the best schools if you are unique.

The nosy 5-year-old test

Do the "nosy 5-year old sister test" to find your "why". She will ask you five times a day, just like a little sister. She asks you "Why?" five times every time you speak to her.

You say, "I'm going out.".

"Why?" she asks.

You reply, "I must go to the shop.".

Why?" she insists.

You respond, "To obtain milk and sugar,".

"Why?" she inquires.

You answer, "So I can bake a cake.".

"Why?" she asks again.

You reply, "Because the store-bought cake has too much icing.". "Why?" she questions.

You admit that it is your mom's birthday tomorrow and she loves my homemade cakes.

Your little sister discovered the true reason why you went to the shop by asking "why?" five times. The same principle can be used to find the reason why you will persevere.

You may not know your "why" but that is perfectly normal. Here's a question to help you think about: Why do I get up in the morning? You may enjoy the hot coffee or chocolate your mom makes in the morning. Or maybe you're passionate about learning more about animal rights or running a better race each day.

Sally, for example, is interested in learning languages. We can ask Sally "Why?" 5x to find out her motivation.

(1) What are you most interested in learning languages? Sally:

To understand a culture you must learn its language. (2) Why is it important to understand other cultures? Sally:

Understanding the culture of another person can help you

to connect with others.

(3) Why is it important for us to get in touch with each other?

Sally: Our technology is so connected, but we are not

connected to being present and making people feel heard. (4) Why is it so important that people feel heard? Sally: Hearing

is the first step in solving problems or gathering

information.

(5) Why is it important that problems are solved? Sally: My

parents had many problems in their marriage. They didn't

know how to or want to solve problems, which led themto get divorced. I want to be a person who perseveres and is part the solution.

This is Sally's motivation to persevere and solve problems. What has your upbringing had to do with your motivation?

Growing up, money chaos was a constant struggle for me. I know how damaging it can be to our relationships. This is why I wanted to be highly employable and attended the top colleges. I will teach you how to make a difference at these top schools.

I want you to be highly employable, so you don't need to worry about finding a job or paying your next utility bill. Instead, you can concentrate on building loving relationships.

Summary

In this chapter you learned that getting into the Ivy League is tough.

From keeping up your grades, working with teachers, serving in after school clubs, getting internships, and studying for the ACT, your life has to be organized, and you have to be disciplined. You also learned that all this energy doesn't just appear, you have to create it by having a strong reason underneath it all, by having a strong, personal "why."

You can start to figure out your "why" by using the "nosy 5year-old test."

Action Steps

Begin to think about your "why", by asking yourself "Why?" 5x Write down your "Why" and place it where you can see it every single day, such as a post-it note in your mirror.

Chapter 5: How To Stand Out To The Ivy League With The Achieve System

You now know that you don't have to do all the same activities as everyone else. You must be unique. You must balance this with advanced classes, test prep, and be aware that it may sometimes be difficult to decide what priority to give.

This is the "being different" part. It's possible you are still wondering "How can I be different?". You can make a difference by putting in a lot of effort and getting to know your teachers. These teachers are the key to your success in school. They can help you pass exams, get into college, and even get letters of recommendation. Next, you will need to find a mentor to help you in your career search. These mentors care about your career and can help with internships or informational interviewing.

Yes. Yes. This book contains a lot information and steps. You have this book and I am here to help you remember them all with just one word: ACHIEVE.

The ACHIEVE system can be used to help you find your way if you are lost. 7 steps to find your standout factor. This system should be used in order to help you prioritize your time. Although you can do both steps simultaneously, it is easier and less stressful to complete step 1 first before moving on to step 2. It is best to focus on only one step at a given time. You can then move on to the next step if you are proficient at this step.

Before the standout system

Before I discovered about the application niche or theme, I struggled with extracurriculars and figuring out if I was on track. I also struggled to distinguish myself from other applicants, particularly Asians with impressive stats.

I felt lost and didn't believe I was enough to be accepted by the Ivy League. I couldn't prioritize my tasks or see a way to get into top colleges.

Because my immigrant family had high hopes, it was difficult. As the oldest child, it was hard for me to disappoint them. It was hard because they kept bringing up other children's achievements, such as Julie's daughter who went to Harvard or Sunny's son who won a national piano award. Do you find this familiar?

Now, I want to help you imagine your life. Since I started the ACHIEVE program, I felt more confident about my future, was less confused, and was able feel that I was on the right path. It was the reason I was able get into Harvard and other prestigious schools such as Dartmouth, UC Berkeley, and Duke. I was so thrilled about it that I shared it to a fellow student who used the system and also got into Harvard early action.

This standout system works for international students too

One of my students was an international student that I had coached. She was concerned about extracurriculars as her school did not have any clubs. She was able to access opportunities from all corners of the globe after putting the ACHIEVE plan in action. These opportunities included a rocket science internship, and other research opportunities. She will undoubtedly be a top applicant to top schools. Imagine what it would be like?

Let me tell you a little bit about myself. I don't have any superpowers or special talents. It's still a struggle for me to figure out what makes me unique and different. This is what I love most about the system: I don't have worry about it anymore!

I will guide you through the steps of my system, which I have developed over many years of coaching students and researching other Ivy League student admissions.

There are 7 steps and corresponding skills you need to master in order to stand out

In the next chapters, I will walk you through each step. You'll also find examples of how it works. The associated skill for each step is shown in brackets.

1. A: As in advanced classes (4-year Advanced Schedule). C:

Perform an activity audit (The Time Audit).

2. H: Help your teacher (The Avocado Toast Method).

3. I: Ignite your interests (Online Outreach) E: Implement your theme (Finding your Theme).

4. V: Validate and validate your credibility (Resume Writing to Impact)

5. E: Get your SAT/ACT exam score (The AccountabilityBuddy). To help you remember the steps in the order they are listed, you can use the acronym "ACHIEVE". You'll find out more about each step and how you can apply it to your plan in the next chapters. Each chapter will include examples from various majors to help you put it into practice.

Summary

In this chapter you were introduced to the concept of ACHIEVE, a system that will help you figure out where you are in the application process and provide skills to help you finish your college application like a boss.

The ACHIEVE system has been proven with students from all backgrounds and will be your ultimate checklist for success. Action Steps

Note the meaning of each letter in the ACHIEVE system With respect for each person, reflect on where you stand.

Part 2 The ACHIEVE System

Chapter 6: Step 1 Of Achieve– Aim For As In Advanced Classes

Each letter in an acronym can help you recall a larger concept. The acronym ACHIEVE stands to stand for "Aim for as in Advanced Classes"

Let's take it one step at a while. Why should you take advanced classes? It's true that it is "easier said then done." This is actually a loophole. Advanced class simply means the subject that interests you most and encourages you to learn more. You don't have to work as hard in your favorite subject. It feels more fun and you get better grades. It doesn't matter if you don't like a subject. You should try to do well in that subject.

Take classes you find interesting

It's something you have probably experienced. Reading about certain topics can make time seem to fly by. You're one minute reading about something that interests you, and then the next, it's over an hour.

Sometimes you may have felt so bored by reading something boring that you thought you would fall asleep. You can't trick anyone into giving you good grades in classes that you don't like.

Good grades are still required in core subjects like English and sciences. You should also take the highest-level courses at your high school. This is partly to show a strict schedule and partly to expose yourself to other types of thinking and subject matter.

A rigorous schedule is a great way to show the Ivy League admissions officers that you can manage multiple deadlines and high-pressure and your commitment to a particular career path.

It's important that you shine in your best classes. However, it is also important to look at the classes of your friends to see how they do. To confirm the accuracy of your program, I recommend that you speak to your guidance counselor.

The "rigor" of the school's classes. Your guidance counselor should consider your schedule as "most rigorous".

If all advanced students in your school are taking 10 AP courses, then you must be meeting the average plus or minus 1. Although it's not an exact measurement, you should at least meet the standards of your school. Your application will be directly compared with those from nearby schools and your own.

Getting into advanced classes

Many people in my neighborhood were shocked to learn that I had been accepted to Harvard. In 4th grade, I recall that gifted students would go off to pursue their advanced curriculum. I stayed behind the normal children.

I was not in the gifted program at elementary school so I wasn't placed in advanced classes at middle school. In 7th grade, I was not in the gifted program, so I was in regular English, not honors, but not in the most advanced math class. It didn't bother me at the time because I didn't know there was a difference.

I was a good student in English class. I did all my homework and participated in class. My 7th grade English teacher suggested that I take the honors English class. I accepted the assessment.

The exam was very strange, as it had multiple choice patterns recognition and spatial intelligence tests. There was a 5-by-5 grid and each square had one circle, star, heart or star. To fill in the empty squares, you had to find the pattern.

I struggled with each question and felt that I knew the answers to all. I was disappointed when I got home. I was frustrated and wondered "How do shapes relate with English?" This test truly measured my intelligence? Unsurprisingly, I discovered that I failed a few months later!

My English teacher saw the hard work I put in to the class, asking lots of questions and staying through breaks. They gave me such a great recommendation that they allowed me to take the advanced class. The main point is that I was allowed to enter the advanced class because of my hard work.

Although "intelligence tests" do not accurately measure your potential, they can have a significant impact on your academic future. Your teachers are the key to getting you into advanced classes.

Another example is my math class. My math class was another example. I failed the intelligence test and had to take a lower-level class. To make matters worse, my 7th grade teacher called out the names of everyone who hadn't written their last names on assignments.

Your last name is not on the paper. My math teacher insisted that you put yourlastname on the papers in middle school.

I was afraid that my poor start might make it difficult for me to get into a good college. It wasn't just me. After that, everyone was afraid of her.

However, later on I needed assistance with a math assignment. My dad was a great help. He solved my math problem in no time and explained every step. Although my dad is extremely smart and has won many academic competitions in China he was not the best at explaining things. We nongeniuses are slower so we need to take things step by step.

After class, I was able to get help from my math teacher. I can still remember the moment when I walked up the ramp to her brown shipping box classroom. The smell of old papers and fresh paint greeted me as I opened the door. I made eye contact to my math teacher who was alone grading. In awkward silence, a ball of crumpled paper appeared to pass in front

us. Finally, I said that I had questions about the assignment.

Her face lit up like the sky parted after a biblical flood and she said, "That is what I'm here to do, honey, to help teach you this!"

She did! She was a kind and sweet lady and showed me many pictures of her nephews and nieces. To make sure that I understood the concepts, I returned several times. She suggested that I might be a good match for the advanced math class in one of our after-school meetings. She stated, "Idon't want you to go, but because you are such an amazing teacher, I do not want you to go."

Great student. I want you to be even more challenging. "I will check on the other course for you," she did. I was accepted into Algebra 2 Honors in 7th grade.

Your teachers are an important resource

It is important to spend time with teachers and help them understand your goals. Teachers will recommend you to higher-level classes if you are diligent and take initiative. Begin by reaching out to your teacher and asking for assistance. It will be amazing how willing they are to help you. You can invite a friend along if you're nervous.

Your guidance counselor

Your guidance counselor is another important resource. I can remember signing up to speak about my class schedule. I was a small fish in the big pond. (I went to a large public high school so there were approximately 400 students per counselor).

It can be difficult to believe that they are so busy or don't want any attention, but it's their job. They are there to assist you with your career, academic, and college planning. The counselor came to my 9th grade class and gave a presentation on how to use the counselor office to create a 4-year plan. I accepted the offer and signed up to create my 4-year plan.

It was quiet when I got to the counselor's office. I expected to see lines of students today, but they weren't there. This surprised me, but I also wondered if it was a good sign. As I entered, I was greeted by Mr. Sklove who was the guidance counselor for last-names starting withC.

J.

He was friendly and made me feel at ease. There were many posters of marathons that he had run as well as some bands that he loved. After getting to know each other, we got to work. Together, we created a 4-year program that included classes at the local community colleges through dual enrollment. Because my high school did not have one, we worked together to create a schedule that allowed me to participate in the community college debate group. They meet twice per week from 1:30pm-4.30pm. My counselor assisted me in approaching my senior year teachers so that I could be off school by 12:01pm to participate in the debate team at the local college. It was amazing!

To help you grow, your counselor and teachers became part of their profession. My high school counselor said that the main reason he was there is to help students. I wish there were more students who came in with questions. I believe that anyone can accomplish anything with the right support. So get to know your teachers and counselors, and impress them with your initiative and determination.

In junior high, I wasn't in the most advanced classes. I was looking for a greater challenge so I took placement exams and worked with my teachers to be more proactive. My teachers were impressed with my performance and recommended me to the highest level to allow me to be accepted into the advanced classes.

It is important to remember that you will also be building your network by doing this. This profession was founded by teachers to support students like you. Your network can help you when you start a club or require a teacher to be the advisor. You may be able to access opportunities that are not available to other students, such as the opportunity to represent the school in the UC Berkeley young worker's rights summit. It can help you obtain the outstanding letters of recommendation that will humanize you during the admissions process.

What if you're not good at communicating with adults?

It is normal to feel intimidated by adults. However, there are two things that can help you overcome this fear. First, be ready with questions. My first meeting with my guidance counselor was when I brought a list full of questions. For example, how do I make an advanced schedule that isn't too overwhelming? What clubs are good for me if I am interested in medicine and law? When I first went to my teachers' break, I brought a few problems that I was having trouble with. Preparation can ease nerves.

Slow down your breathing. Your brain records data about how you feel, so if your heart rate starts to race, your brain may start to panic and you might fall ill. Before approaching teachers or giving a talk, 4-7-8 breathing can be a useful technique. You need to inhale for four seconds, hold it for seven, and then exhale for eight. Repeat 10 times. This will lower your heart rate, allowing you to speak normally to your teachers.

Skill: The 4-year advanced schedule

Getting an advanced schedule - your plan

Your master plan and timeline is the 4-year advanced schedule. It can be reduced depending on how many years you are still in high school. This document will be a reference that you refer to repeatedly. It can also help you start many conversations, such as with your teachers to explain why you want to take an advanced class. You can also discuss with your counselor how you can find additional classes that are related to your interests, and even internship opportunities.

Begin by meeting with your counselor. This is a good time to meet, especially if it's not busy season for finalizing classes. You can create a 4-year plan that includes electives and advanced classes. Next, adjust every year.

You can use the 4-year advanced program to represent yourself in school if you haven't been in advanced classes:

1) Ask your advanced class teacher to reserve a spot. There are two main guides in school. Your high school counselor is the first and your teacher in advanced classes is the second. You can get to know both of them and discuss your desire to take on a greater challenge. Consider dual enrollment at your local communitycollege, or online classes like APEX. APEX is used by one of my students to access AP classes that aren't available at her school or don't fit into her schedule. You can also study for AP exams by yourself using resources such as UC Scout.

2) Placement tests are required. Some schools allow you to choose any class you like, while others require you to pass a test in order to be eligible for advanced classes. My

high school counselor told me a story about a student trying to get into advanced math classes. The advanced math teacher wasn't sure he was ready because he had only received a B in his previous math class. He was recommended by his counselor to take the placement exam at the community college. He took the test and did well enough in his community college class to be able to take an advanced math class at high school the following year.

Do not let anyone, teacher included, stop you from achieving your goals, regardless of whether they are family members, friends, or enemies. There are many other paths that can lead you to your goal.

Aiming for As

You've now learned how to get into advanced classes. Here are some tips to help you not only survive, but thrive. Students often ask me whether it is better to get an "A" in a regular class than a "B" in an advanced class. This is not the right question to ask if you are looking for a school with top students who take advanced classes. It's obvious that advanced classes are better than regular classes. So, a better question is: How do you get an A grade in advanced classes?

My teacher told me that we would be taking a test on The Odyssey in my freshman year of Honors English. I was panicked as I hadn't even read one page. I hated reading assignments and relied heavily upon summary sites such as Shmoop and Sparknotes to help me understand. I returned home to try to understand the old translation stories, but fell asleep quickly.

After flipping through the many boring pages, I thought to myself "Ah Man, I'm never going get through this", I thought to myself.

I decided to try an online quizzes method of studying for the test. I searched for "Odyssey" and found tons of questions and even a practice test. To help me understand the themes and characters, I started Quizlet. Then I discovered other quizzes that dealt with the plot. Soon, I was ready to take the 100-question quiz. I got an excellent 85. I made a note of the questions that I didn't understand and went back through the descriptions to ensure I had the correct answer.

My exam was the next day. As my English teacher administered the exams, I was anxious.

"Exams face-down until I say so," said my English teacher with short gray hair, no glasses and no frames. You can now start the exam. Keep your eyes on the paper.

I scanned the exam carefully and pondered my fate over the next hour. I was shocked. I was stunned when I flipped through the 100 questions feverishly and found that it was exactly the same test I had taken online. Jackpot. The test was easy and I passed it in record time, looking like a boss.

This exam taught me that online quizzes can really help to improve your knowledge and make it easier to pass the next one. There are some methods that are more efficient than others for studying for exams. Flashcards and memory devices such as mnemonics are great for classes that have a lot of terminology. This mnemonic, Kings Play Chess on Flat Green Squares, helped me remember my 7th grade science class's taxonomy rank (kingdom, phylums, classes, orders, families, genus and species). You can also set things to song. Because my 8th grade teacher made us recite the names of US presidents to Yankee Doodle's tune, I can still recall them. Make studying enjoyable by being creative!

Learning styles

Everybody is different in their learning style. Learning by doing is how I learn best. I can recall sitting in Calculus class and not understanding what my math teacher was saying. Although my math teacher was the best at the school, I am not an auditory or visual learner. Learning by doing is how I learn. I do the math problems and test myself using online quizzes. I also use flashcards.

Finding your learning style can help you make your study more effective. There are four types of learning styles that make up the acronym VARK. They are visual, auditory and reading/writing. [11]

Visual learners learn best when they use diagrams and charts in their studies. Auditory learners learn best when the material is recited aloud to them, such as in a lecture. Writing-oriented learners who are interested in reading and writing benefit from reviewing slides and taking notes. My kinesthetic learners, like me, do well using flashcards and hands-on learning such as in a science laboratory. You can use YouTube videos, flashcards, songs, word mnemonics such as PEMDAS or flashcards to discover your own style. You can mix it all to find the best.

Your syllabus

The playbook for good grades is your syllabus. You should carefully read it to learn the rules. You might find that quizzes and tests make up 80% of your grade, while homework makes up 20%. If I was you, I would study the test questions to improve my test-taking abilities. On the first exam, my mentality is to be able to comprehend the type of questions that will be asked on the next one. You can improve your ability to predict what will be on each exam and how you can study accordingly.

Your ability to obtain a grade buffer (a.k.a. extra credit) might be revealed in your syllabus. Important is the date of the exams on the syllabus. You can set reminders for yourself to study for exams a week before the exam to ensure you have enough time to absorb all the information and are less stressed about cramming. Google Calendar allows you to set up alerts on your smartphone so that you don't have to cram for exams.

Once you have completed your syllabus and set reminders on the calendar for the major test dates, you can create ways to track your grades. You can improve your grades by keeping track of your grades. It's better to detect problems early than later.

Your cure for a slipping grade

1) You must return any lost or missing assignments. Sometimes, you lose things even though you have given it back. Attend the teacher's office at least once a week.

2) Monitor your grades.

It will improve your comprehension of the material by getting to know your teachers. You can also learn more about the teacher and your character, which is a huge advantage if you need a recommendation letter. Exams, feedback and essays can be reviewed to help you adapt your study to the requirements of the test.

Sometimes teachers will post your grades. But sometimes, you have to do it yourself.

You can make your own grade book so you know what assignments you submitted and which exams you passed. It's amazing how many mistakes can be made by simple human errors.

ACHIEVE in action - English example

Imagine your parents reading the New York Times every morning as you grow up. Your parents are always there to explain the international section to you. Although you aren't sure of your future career, you are passionate about English so you decide to get a bachelor's degree in English. You are aware that there are many great writers who apply to top schools. So you use the ACHIEVE program to ensure that you stand out.

Step 1 - Aim for As in Advanced Classes

Step one is a positive step. You're taking all of the AP classes and getting excellent grades. Perhaps you even have decided to take non-fiction writing classes at your local college.

Step 2 - Conduct an Activity Audit

Step two is when you realize there are three things you don't enjoy and that consume a lot of your time. You may have loved playing volleyball, but you now find that yoga is better for you. In ninth grade, you were struggling with math so your parents sent you to a tutoring center. However, you learned how to do math on your own and don't need the help anymore. Although you loved debate, you are comfortable enough to speak in public and prefer writing. You make the difficult but wise decision to stop participating in these activities.

Step 3 - Help your Teacher Help You

Step three is when you begin going to your English teacher's office hours. She tells you that she wants to start a student paper but can't find the right person to do it. You tell her you are up for it and you work together with your counselor to make this a reality.

Step 4 - Ignite your Interests

Next, reach out to role models in non-fiction, such as journalists who wrote in the papers that your parents read. After four months of perseverance, you finally get an interview with one of these journalists.

Step 5 - Execute your Theme

Also, you will start writing every day for the newspaper to improve your writing skills. You keep in touch with the journalist after your interview. When one of their articles is published, you support them and send celebratory emails.

Step 6 - Validate your Credibility

During this time, you're researching writing competitions and entering all the non-fiction ones. Your mentor and your English teacher will give you feedback before you submit your essays. If you win one of the competitions held by foreign services, you will be awarded a trip.

DC.

You and your mentor happen to be in DC so you set up a coffee meet to get to know one another. Your mentor gives you the opportunity to contribute to a large article. Accept it with open arms. Once the article has been published, you save it for your college application.

Step 7 - Earn your Target SAT / ACT score

You decide to take the SAT at the end of your junior year. To help you with the practice tests, you find a study partner. You achieve your target score of 1550 after 50 practice tests.

You can be admitted to Stanford and UPenn as well as many other top schools!

Summary

In step 1 of ACHIEVE, you learned the importance of getting into the most advanced classes that your school has to offer.

You learned some of the main ways to get your teachers and counselors to help you in this process, and it all starts with creating a 4-year plan.

Finally, you learned some tips to do well in your classes and earn your As.

Action Steps

Take the most advanced classes in your school

In most classes, you can get as With your counselor, create a 4-year plan

Chapter 7: Step 2 Of Achieve - Conduct An Activity Audit

After you have focused your efforts on developing good study habits in order to score high marks in advanced classes, let us now look at the biggest obstacle that prevents students from standing out: a lack of time. You may be surprised at how many activities you accumulate by going through your list. It's similar to how you find out how much stuff you have when you move.

Here is my list of activities for junior year:

School Newspaper Club

Academic Decathlon

Key Club community service

National Honor Society

Cross-country

Youth Commission

Health Occupation Students of America

Giant Steps Therapy offers volunteer opportunities for disabled children

Debate Club

Internships

Of course, none of these activities is inherently harmful. Too many things can cause us to lose our focus. Focusing on one thing at a time allows us to get deeper than if we try to do everything. Greg McKeown has a great book called Essentialism: A Disciplined Pursuit Of Less. It will help you understand why less is better. I realized that I needed to cut down on activities and be more focused when I decided to go to Harvard. I focused on debate and internships. It worked well for me. The key to this is that I was able learn more and make more impact by focusing on just a few projects.

It's not an easy task, I know. You may be pushed by your friends to join their classes and clubs. It's tempting to spend time with your friends, but it's not right for you. You will hear from your parents about the volunteer trip all the other children are taking. Although you don't want your parents to be disappointed, it is not the right time for you. Your English teacher will encourage your participation in the high school newspaper. Although you hate writing, it is something that will make your resume stand out. To all of them, say "Thanks, but it's no for me."

Think about all the things that consume your time. You can even write them down. Take the time to go through each activity. Do you find this an "hell-yes," activity? If so, you might want to cut it. Cross-country is worth the time and effort? Is it a joy? If not, Marie Kondo it.

Activities often outlive their purpose. Running was something I did to spend time with my best friend in ninth grade. After the year ended, she moved away but I kept running. I stopped running in eleventh grade because I was bored with it. You must learn to manage your time well if you want to be noticed. It is easy to see why students who come to me to coach have such difficulty standing out. These are the most successful kids in their group.

Why do they struggle to stand out? They are too busy! It's because they are so busy. They have to do the homework for advanced classes and SAT prep. Then, they also have to manage their family responsibilities, such as community service, school clubs, and family responsibilities. These students aren't able to create personal projects or pursue hobbies that will make them stand out from the rest.

Skill: The Time Audit

The key is called an "Activity Audit"

What are you doing with your time? Let's not waste our time wondering where it went. Make a list of all the activities you do and take as much detail as possible. My time was spent mostly in lectures and homework for the many AP classes that I was taking. Ask yourself if you enjoy the subject or activity. Is it in line with your future plans?

That was the moment I realized I had difficulty remembering facts from lectures. It wasn't my fault. I attended a large public school with a strong faculty. It was all about my learning style. Learning is not done by listening and watching, but by practicing and doing. I could spend hours in math class, and still not feel that I had learned anything. It was easy for me to solve the examples on my own, which helped me retain the information I had lost from the hour-long lectures. Reflection and online learning style tests can help you discover how you learn best.

I realized that I needed to be more independent in my studies and was able to miss lectures for my extracurriculars. (I used to travel a lot for debate). Because they were more self-guided and suited my learning style better, I chose to take classes at the local community college. The summer semester I spent there counted towards my high school academic year, which allowed me to have a lot more time in my regular school day.

Ask your counselor at high school about similar programs (also known as dual enrollment) with the local community college.

How to do a "Class Time Audit"

I recommend that you take the most difficult classes, such as honors, IB or AP. It's perfectly acceptable to choose an easier AP class or regular class if it is not a core course, or relevant to your career goals.

English, Math and Foreign Language are the core classes. You should take the more difficult classes. Top schools such as the Ivy League require that high school students have at least three years experience in a foreign language. You can choose to learn the more time-consuming languages like Spanish if languages are not your main focus.

Be aware of the time it will take to choose classes. Ask teachers and upperclassmen to give their opinions. AP Statistics, for example, was less time-consuming at my school than AP Calculus BC. If your career goals do not include hard maths, you should consider AP Stats.

If you want to become a doctor as your career goal, it is important that you take more difficult science classes like AP Biology and Chemistry. You can also choose to take non-science classes such as Computer Science or History if you are not interested in science.

I was a freshman when I first heard about how time-consuming and difficult AP World History would prove to be. The 500+ pages of the massive, shiny textbook were intimidating. I was not a natural history fan nor interested in it so I chose to study regular World History. This was an important decision that allowed me to spend my time on other activities.

Next, do an "Extracurricular Time Audit"

My long list of extracurriculars made me realize that I was exactly the same person as the honors students. All of us were in the same clubs: journalism, honor society, key club and academic decathlon.

The same questions I asked in class audit, I also asked myself. Do I enjoy these activities?" Do these activities align with my future plans?

In truth, I didn't enjoy many of these activities. As most of my classmates, i paid honor society dues and participated in these clubs to help me look good on college applications. I was unable to stand out among the thousands of applicants.

So I quit journalism and academic decathlon to concentrate on my strengths.

It can be hard to quit

It's hard to leave a club when you have people counting on you. The look on the face of my journalism teacher when I announced that I was leaving the journalism club is still vivid in my mind. Her red cheeks turned to a frown of disbelief and resentment.

She replied, "I don't know why you're doing this." You were trained to replace senior editors and be THE copy editor.

I replied, "While I value your time in journalism, and your training, it's not for you." I must make more time for debate.

Although it was difficult to leave journalism, I felt an immense sense of relief as I left the classroom.

It's a great way to free up time by quitting any activities that aren't relevant to your career goals or interests. You will be able to make the most of this extra time and explore your interests to create a project that really helps you stand out.

ACHIEVE in action - Business example

Imagine you're certain you want to be an entrepreneur. You remember your parents selling items on eBay and Craigslist as a child. They even tried to sell used cars. There are many talented applicants who are interested in the business world, so it is important to find a way that you stand out.

Step 1- Aim for As in Advanced Classes

To ensure that your ACHIEVE plan is on the right path, you work step by step. You create a 4-year plan for highschool where you will be taking all the AP classes that work within your schedule and are relevant to your business economics major. You decide to enroll in Marketing 101 and Basic Finance classes at your local community college.

Step 2 - Conduct an Activity Audit

Next, you will move on to cutting activities. Since you were 9th grade, you tried to do everything. After realizing how difficult medical school was, your decision to stop being a journalist, community service club member, and HOSA president is made.

Step 3 - Help your Teacher Help You

You then form a partnership with your economics teacher who is also a small-business owner and whose family runs a small restaurant in the center

of the city. You decide it would be great to start a school business club.

Step 4 - Ignite your Interests

You establish your business club with your economics instructor as your advisor. Next, you contact your local chamber to find speakers for your club. Interview them to find out their most pressing issues. It becomes clear that financing Spanish business owners is a major problem.

Step 5 - Execute your Theme

You agree to take on this project. To provide Spanish resources, you partner with your Economics professor, local banks, or the Chamber of Commerce.

Step 6 - Validate your credibility

Local newspapers and television stations love to feature people who give back to their communities. They hear about you through the Chamber of Commerce. These news clips can be saved for your senior year application.

Step 7 - Earn your Target SAT / ACT score

You don't have the money to pay for a tutor for the ACT standardized test, so you sign up for a Boot Camp online. There you can take practice tests for the ACT. Your target score of 34 is achieved.

You can be admitted to Cornell and UPenn.

Summary

In order to stand out, you need the time to do so.

An Activity Audit will allow you to free up time for the next steps

of the ACHIEVE program. This audit will help you to eliminate classes and activities that aren't relevant to your future goals, or don't interest you anymore.

Quitting can be hard, but being overwhelmed by a laundry list of activities is worse.

Any time you feel overwhelmed and don't have enough time, do an activity audit.

Action Steps

Conduct a "class time audit"

Perform an "extracurricular time audit". Reduce your schedule to just 1-2 activities ("Do less but better")

Chapter 8: Step 3 Of Achieve - Help Your Teacher Help You

High school senior year, I was voted Teacher's Pet. It is most likely that I will return as a teacher. I enjoyed tutoring and teaching others so the second label was logical. The teacher's pet label, however, wasn't so logical.

I was not the best student. This is because my teachers used to tell me who scored the highest on essays and test scores, and I was not one of them. In terms of attendance, I felt like I was the worst student among the top 10. People thought I was the best friend of teachers, as I would stay to chat with them every break. Because I was always missing class for debate tournaments or internships, I was actually always making up assignments.

Looking back, I realized that most students don't speak to their teachers other than when they are called upon in class. This is a problem in college admissions for several reasons. First, if you have never had contact with your teacher you won't be able to share anything about you. You'll also look like all the other applicants.

Second, you will do better in class if your teacher is familiar. This is because you're more likely to ask for help when you need. There have been teachers that were intimidating and who you would not dare to go to alone during breaks to ask a question.

Teachers can be your mentors, offering wisdom and practical advice as you move forward in your career. Let's say that you are passionate about biology and you do your best in your biology class. Your teacher expresses interestin doing research and tells you later that she has a unique opportunity for you.

You receive an email from a local biology professor requesting a high school intern. After you approve, she sends you a recommendation. You are invited to interview. Your teacher offers to practice interviewing with your. The interview goes well and you are selected for this research opportunity. You can ask your teachers to help you write letters supporting prestigious, competitive summer programs or full-ride scholarships.

Getting to know your teachers

In 7th grade, Spanish was my first language. I decided to learn more and volunteer to help my Spanish teacher.

He was a friendly Polish man with glasses and a beard. His name was 7-syllables long. We used to practice saying it so often. I offered to help him grade papers and organize papers during one break. He was astonished and accepted my offer. Each week, I would grade homework assignments and test papers and organize papers for class.

The work was enjoyable because I got to see what teachers do outside of the classroom. I also learned more about the journey of my Spanish teacher.

In 8th grade I was the same teacher's assistant volunteer role as my Geometry teacher. I also learned about the salaries of teachers, tenure (it's a permanent job contract), how teachers spend their time, and what Geometry is like.

This helped me to feel more at ease with my teachers. It also made me realize how important it was for them to help students. This allowed me to ask for clarifications on complicated concepts and felt more comfortable with my teachers so it was never too late to get back from exam failures or poor grades.

How to become friends with your teachers

You can build a friendship with your teachers by helping them in any way you can. For example, volunteering to help them get guineas or taking part in class. How would you feel if you presented to the class and nobody responded to it? You can prepare questions for the class ahead of time if you're nervous about participating. Teachers love those who take part!

Ask your teacher if you'd be interested in volunteering to help as a teacher assistant. It's important to make it easy for your teacher to say yes. You can list ways you can help, such as creating flashcards, study guides, and helping organize papers or digital documents.

When you begin volunteering regularly, take the time to get acquainted with them. How did they get to be a teacher? What are their hobbies? Your teachers will be able to learn more about you and your dreams.

One of my students who I coach is passionate about girls' education in Southeast Asia. Her 10th grade English teacher was thrilled to hear that she was going to Harvard for a conference on the state of women in Southeast Asia.

This will demonstrate to admissions officers that the student is passionate about the topic. Side note: Normally, you will ask for letters from 11th-grade teachers. However, if you speak to your 10th-grade teacher regularly, such as if she has been involved in your club for three years, it may be acceptable. It is important to show dedication over time. Get to know your teachers, and keep them informed about your extracurricular activities!

Skill: The Avocado Toast Method

How can you get to know your teachers, and make them your mentors? How can you get to know your classmates? Give them value. Avocado toast is something they will love if you make it every day. You give them compliments on their teaching every class if they seem low in motivation due to the virtual learning environment.

Avocado toast is similar to growing avocado trees. [12] The first step is to determine the right conditions. For example, when your teacher is happy. Next, you will plant the seed and have a conversation about it with your teacher. You'll then need to care for the plant by giving it water every now and again, as well as fertilizing it once in a while. This can be done with your teacher by attending class regularly and going to office hours. You will soon

reap the benefits of avocados and a great friendship with your teacher, who will guide you in your career path and write you a letter of recommendation. It is based on the principle that you can win someone's trust by making them smile every day. It doesn't need to be avocado toast or expensive, but it must be thoughtful and specific for the person. It could be as simple to actively participate in every class if we are talking about teachers.

This is not a quick way to make a fortune. You won't find anyone who will mentor you or give you any meaningful advice. This is not a place for beginners. It takes time but it is worth it.

What can you do to ensure you provide value? Ask the person. Ask the person how you can help and what their greatest challenge is. Next, brainstorm ways you can make it easier. Your teacher might say that participation in class is her greatest challenge. With your teacher's support, you could help to research ways to increase participation.

Avocado toast is all about being present every day and adding small amounts of value into someone's lives.

ACHIEVE in action - Pre-med example

Let's say you dream of becoming a doctor. As a child, you would travel with your dad, who was suffering from a variety of health problems, such as diabetes and high blood pressure. You also helped translate for your immigrant father. Although it was daunting and involved a lot of responsibility you learned a lot from your experience at the hospital. You also made friends with the doctors.

The Ivy League is a large institution that accepts premed applicants. You need to be able to stand out. To make sure you're on the right path, you will go through the steps in ACHIEVE.

Step 1 - Aim for As in Advanced Classes

You'll find that you have completed step one and are now taking advanced classes such as AP chem and AP bio. Also, you've learned that flashcards are a great way to learn and that YouTube can help you understand complex concepts. After you have achieved As in your classes you can look at the next step of the ACHIEVE program.

Step 2 - Conduct an Activity Audit

Conducting an activity audit is the second step. You will see that there are many activities that consume your time. You email the club presidents to inform them that there are other priorities and you can't continue.

Step 3 - Help your Teacher Help You

You now have the time to use the lunches that you used to attend club meetings for your biology teacher. You discover that you can help your biology teacher and other students by sharing fun YouTube videos that explain complex concepts. Your work is appreciated by your classmates and teachers.

Step 4 - Ignite your Interests

You then work on your passions to find your theme. Finally, you contact your doctor for an informational interview. You ask her about volunteer opportunities for high school students. She tells you that she cannot hire you because you are under 18, but that you can volunteer at the local teens health clinic. You receive an email from her indicating that the local clinic is seeking social media support.

YouTube videos are a great way to learn social media basics, even if you're not a social-media superstar. You realize the dangers of vaping while volunteering at a teen clinic. One of your ideas is to launch a social media campaign to raise awareness about the dangers of vaping. You reach out to top researchers to help you build your posts.

Step 5 - Execute your Theme

You form a close friendship with one of the researchers, and she offers

you a position as a research assistant.

Step 6 - Validate your credibility

Your research can lead to your name being published in a publication. Your hard work in the Stop Vaping Social Media Campaign has resulted in your local newspaper emailing you to publish your story. This news clipping can be saved for senior year college applications.

Step 7 - Earn your Target SAT / ACT score

You spend three months preparing to take the ACT at the end of your

junior year. Your target score is 35 out of 36.

Brown, Columbia and other top schools are yours.

Summary

In step 3 of ACHIEVE, you learned that it's important to get to know your teachers so they can understand how to help you. Through the "Avocado ToastMethod" of adding value, you develop a strong bond with your teachers. Because of that, you not only feel comfortable asking questions when youdon't understand something but you also start participating in class and enjoying school more.

Later, when you need a club advisor or a letter of recommendation, you know you can count on your teachers.

Action Steps

Participate in each class at least once (it could be asking questions).

Take note of ways that you can make the life of your teacher easier Talk to your teacher about your career choices.

Chapter 9: Step 4 Of Achieve - Ignite Your Interests

I was 14 years old when I entered the high school career centre, which was located in the academic counseling offices. I began to talk to Mrs. K, a tall, thin career counselor who had a blonde hairstyle. I was welcomed to the career center by her and she explained that it was available for all high school students.

I was curious about the new location and asked her if there were any resources to help me figure out my future career goals. She smiled and explained about aptitude tests, which are quizzes that help you determine what career is right for you based upon your interests.

I requested to take one and sat down at the nearby table to learn more. We discovered that law practice could be a good match after completing a short quiz. Although I was conflicted by my desire to become a doctor, Mrs. K suggested that I could combine both. I was intrigued when she told me her brother was a pharmacist lawyer.

"Oh!" I exclaimed. I can do medical law."

She didn't know that I would be coming into Harvard as a freshman

and telling everyone, "I want international pharmaceutical lawyers." (International because I love languages too. Because I was so precise, my college classmates still recall that.

Mrs. K was impressed by my enthusiasm about combining my interest in medicine and law. She suggested that I speak to Mr. L. He is a historian who had been a lawyer before. I thanked Mrs. K and left her office feeling excited to pursue this new career path.

That day is still a vivid memory of mine. My most vivid memory is that it was a rainy afternoon and my mom patiently waited after school for us. My mom was supportive and allowed me to stay late. I wanted to thank her. Your parents are very special. They are there to help you.

How to figure out what you want to do

1) Take an aptitude exam.

These can help you discover what is important to you. However, you should take them with a grain. As you discover more about yourself, your career goals will change and evolve.

If the job description suggests you as an architect, but you don't want to do that, continue down the list until you find other careers that are more appealing. These are not magical Harry Potter Sorting Hats. You must interpret the results and decide what you want.

These are just a few resources I recommend. Feel free to explore more:

Minnesota State Career Cluster Interest Survey

My Next Move Interest Profiler

MAPP(tm), Career Assessment Test

2) Make a list of all your interests. Do not worry about how long the list is. What classes have you enjoyed? What are the things I want to do on Saturday mornings? It doesn't have to be academic at first. It's important that you are truly interested in the subject.

You might enjoy watching videos about how to care succulent plants or you may be very interested in botany and the biology of plants. Maybe you enjoy coaching junior high soccer at weekends.

3) Find the intersections.

I was attracted to medicine and law so I explored medical law. Is there anything you could add to your list? Do you have an interest in neuroscience or swimming? Do you enjoy history and drawing? Draw the possible intersections.

4) To explore more, pick one of these intersections. Perhaps it was neuroscience and swimming. You could also look into the

neuroscience behind swimming. You can also look into art history if you're interested in history and drawing.

5) Spend at least 15 minutes each day pursuing your interests. Your interest is like the seed of a plant. To make it grow, you must nurture it.

Give it energy and your time. These topics can be found in books at your local library. You can browse blogs or watch YouTube videos about your interests. Find out the trends and common terms that are used in the field.

Interview professionals in your field

Once you feel confident in your knowledge of botany, you can reach out to other people in the field and find out if they are open to working with you.

You might be a fan of innovation and a fast-paced work environment. So you interview local marketing managers to find out if they include this in their culture. Perhaps you enjoy drawing and would like to have some personal time. However, interviewing journalists reveals that you are often limited in your ability to keep up with deadlines.

Throughout my professional and academic career, I have conducted hundreds of interviews. This will allow you to see what it's like to work in this field. Is it something they love? How did they get there? What are their dayto-day responsibilities?

Junior year at college I was very interested in luxury retail. I reached out to people who worked in these roles at Chanel, Louis Vutton, and Burberry. These interviews taught me how important it was to have experience in stores. They are the ones who run the cash registers and drive sales. I applied to all the luxury stores in Boston, and I got a job at Louis Vuitton. My retail experience made me stand out in the application process for internships. I ended up being hired by Bloomingdales during my junior year of college. Interviews can prepare you for entry into the field, and could lead to other opportunities.

Use your personal network

Ask everyone you know. My career counselor connected me to a high school teacher who was a lawyer. One of my students was interested and remembered meeting an aerospace engineer at a family event.

It is worth asking yourself: Who do I know who is well connected? It could be a teacher who knows everyone in town or your best friend who volunteers with many programs.

If you're interested in Chemistry, for example, and are looking to do research, talk to your counselors, teachers, and family members to find out if there are any Chemistry professors or research opportunities.

It is common to hear, "I don't know anyone, but... I'll keep you in my mind." It can be worthwhile to hear someone say, "Actually I do know someone.".

It is all about creating relationships. You just have to keep trying. When asking for assistance, be kind and respectful. Although they may not be able immediately to assist you, you can ask them to keep in touch with you if they do.

After you have exhausted all the people you know, it's time to start reaching out to others. These are known as "cold leads" in sales. However, warm leads are more likely to be interviewed for a job. There are also many cold leads available, so there is no limit to the possibilities.

How to interview people you don't know

Skill: Online Outreach

Online Outreach is when you send an email to someone you don't know, but would like to. This is also called "cold emailing" and "networking." You won't bombard someone with tons of questions, just as you wouldn't text someone you don't know with a long list of requests. It's really one question: "I'm interested in your career, can you tell me more about how it got started?" People love to share their stories, so let them. This approach can also be used to get to know your teachers. Begin with curiosity and respect by asking questions!

Online Outreach emails are especially helpful when you want to reach out to professors, alumni, and the president. Anyone can use the Online Outreach email. You can cold email a University president to get in touch with him. You might be more specific and email a professor from the department you are interested in. But you get my point. Cold emailing is a great way to reach out to anyone. The worst thing that could happen is not hearing back. You get ignored. You get lost in the jumbled emails of busy people. It can be very frustrating to ignore emails you have spent so much effort on, but it isn't that bad.

It doesn't matter if they never reply, it will still be okay. Plus, there are tons of people out there. It's a numbers game. The person who sends the most messages will get the most responses and opportunities. They will also feel less doubtful. There are techniques that I use to ensure that I get a response. It's important to be persistent and positive when meeting new people.

To simplify email outreach, I will focus on one way to use this technique. This is also a great way to meet people and get internships or jobs. It can also help you build great relationships. Cold emailing is a great way to obtain informational interviews. Informational interviews can help you get anywhere. Cali, my student tried it out and got three remote internships in mechanical engineering in just one summer. She was working on rocket parts before the end of the summer. It wasn't a joke. All because she cold emailed dozens companies and research websites she found online.

Mentors can be reached online by people who are interested in your job. Mentors can be found at schools, clubs and in the teams you are a member of. The better, the more diverse. I prefer to have multiple mentors in different fields, rather than one mentor who deals with all my problems.

This is something you'll learn about college. However, most college students I spoke to said that the best thing about college was being exposed to other ways of thinking and perspectives from students around the globe. You will find your next career path by gaining different perspectives from mentors.

Finding Mentors

Looking back, I can see how entering the career office made me more interested in medical law. But, more importantly, it opened up a friendship with a mentor. Mentors are key to your success. Mentors can help you find new opportunities and mentors. This is how it worked for me. Mrs. K suggested that I contact Mr. L, a school history teacher who was a lawyer, and so I did.

I was unable to find his classroom. Upon entering, I saw a tall, slender man with a balding head and a brown coat. He was engaging in deep conversation with an older, but more elegant, AP English teacher.

I approached them sheepishly and respectfully interrupted their conversation to introduce me. I told him that Mrs. K, his career counselor, recommended that I speak to him because I was interested to become a medical attorney. He smiled and said, "I don't practice law anymore, but fortunately I have a friend who does medical law only 20 minutes from me." He can be reached at me if you would like?" I quickly replied, "That would absolutely be incredible!"

My mom and I were able to meet with Mr. L after Mr. L reached out to his friend. We met up with his friend at the law office a week later and set up an informal, unpaid internship in which I would shadow him and file legal documents. Also, I would do research once per week.

Perhaps you're interested in architecture but don't know anyone in the field.

Reaching out to professionals is possible in three ways. You can first use social media platforms like LinkedIn to reach professionals in your field and send them a personal message expressing interest in their career path.

To connect with them, you can send a brief message. You don't need to pay anything to send them a LinkedIn message. Click "Connect" on their profile and "Add a Note."

Here is a LinkedIn template. Due to character limitations, you need to keep it brief:

Hi [Name],

I am currently a sophomore in grade e.g. at [your highschool] and I am interested in marketing, [industry]. I would like to know if [industry] is something you enjoy and if it's something you recommend. I would appreciate a quick call or coffee for a 15-20 minute discussion to find out more. Thank you!

[Your Name]

You can also find their email addresses online (many professors have them online) and send a brief email to them.

Here is a template that you can use to create an email:

Hi [Name],

I am currently a sophomore in grade e.g. at [your highschool] and am interested in marketing. I was impressed by your research on [research paper topic, e.g. MEMS and sensors materials] so I wanted to get in touch.

I am interested in your career path in [industry e.g. engineering] and [something notable about their career, such as "your profession change from a management consultant to an Engineer professor".

I was wondering if it would be possible to have a quick coffee call with you to discuss your views on the industry, and if you recommend that we pursue [industry, E.g. engineering]!

Thanks,

[Your Name]

Quantity can help

This should be done for at least 10 people. While many people will not respond, a few will. These few people are your doors to new opportunities. Thank them for their time and make sure to take as many notes during the meeting or call as possible.

Make sure you have a list with specific questions for them and their industry before you call.

An informational interview is not the best time to apply for a job or internship. It is important to establish a rapport with the person you are interviewing and to provide value. This is your chance to impress them by your initiative and insider knowledge. In your

"Thank You" note, you will ask them about internships and job shadowing opportunities. These are some great questions that you can ask:

I noticed that X is happening in the job industry. What are your thoughts on it?

Why did you choose this career?

How did you get this job?

What would you say about the ideal person for this job? What is the best way to prepare for a job like yours? What should I do in highschool?

What do you wish someone would have told you before you started this career?

How do you think this job will change over the next 10 years?

What's it like to work at your company? What's the day -to-day

like?

What's the biggest challenge in your job?

What is the greatest pro and con to your job?

If the chemistry is right, you can thank them at the end of the call and ask them if they know of other opportunities or colleagues who would be willing to speak with you. You never know who might be able to introduce you to others in your field.

You should contact the company within 1-2 days to thank them for their call and mention that you would love to shadow a job or intern.

Here's an example of a "Thank You Note":
Dear [Name],

Thank you for taking the time and talking to me about [job title] today/yesterday. It was a pleasure to have had this conversation with you and [hear/learn about] the [thing that we discussed]. Also, it was great to learn about [something you discussed].

I'm very excited about this job and believe that my interests in [share pertinent aspects of your past] would make me a great match for the position. [job title].

If you have the opportunity, I would love to shadow a job or intern. Thank you again,

[Your Name]

You will be able to shadow, intern or gain valuable mentorship if you

do this with enough professionals.

Joining interest groups or organizations is the third way to get interviews. Let's say you are interested and passionate about animal science. Are there any local museums for animal science or professional groups for vets? Contact them to see if they are available for you to join a meeting.

Interviews will give you a better idea of your career path and help you choose the right extracurriculars to add to your application.

You can still make progress if you decide that this topic is not for you. It is important to get to know yourself better. My local university gave me a chemistry internship and I realized that Ididn't like lab work. This would have taken up a lot of my time if my goal was to study pre-med.

Perhaps you find your passion and it becomes your hobby! Bingo! You're one step closer to being a member of the Ivy League. Your passion will become your passion portfolio. I'll explain this in the next chapter.

ACHIEVE in action - Art example

Imagine you are passionate about Art. Your parents are passionate about photography, and your older sister is an artist. They love your creativity and you are certain that you would enjoy a career as an artist.

The creative world is crowded. It can be hard to stand out. To make sure that you have the right strategy, you use the ACHIEVE tool.

Step 1 - Aim for As in Advanced Classes

You realize that your math grade is in dire need of a makeover. You visit your teacher's office and discuss ways you can better understand math concepts. You might also want to go over all of your incorrect answers on homework assignments or exams each week. This will help you feel better about math.

Step 2 - Conduct an Activity Audit

You will discover that you are in clubs that don't excite you when you do an activity audit. You may have enjoyed the mentorship program but don't like it in virtual. You may have thought that maybe you wanted a career as a doctor. So you joined the health sciences club. But now you realize that this is not what you want. These clubs were closed to you so that you can spend more time on the things that will make you stand out.

Step 3 - Help your Teacher Help You

You had an idea to start an art therapy club. This idea is brought up by your teacher. She is very excited and you work with your guidance counsel to complete the required paperwork to start the club. You think of other clubs you could partner with like the senior citizens' health club and brainstorm ways to help them.

You can create a social media account and post helpful information about art therapy to spread the word about this club. You can use these to help you with creative writing, quick drawing, coloring books for relaxation, and many other things. This helps you to quickly gain popularity in your school or community and help you recruit club officers to help get this off the ground.

Step 4 - Ignite your Interests

After the club has been established and you have attended a few events, you begin to contact local graphic designers and photographers to find out more about the industry and ways you can get in. Interviews reveal that having a strong portfolio of work is one of the most difficult things to do in order to break into the industry. Unfortunately, many young artists are not able to get feedback on their portfolios, so they end up being rejected for a lot.

Step 5 - Execute your Theme

The next step is to brainstorm possible solutions and then follow up with those you interviewed to find out if they are open to helping. One idea that stood out was to have a portfolio review once a month where artists could submit their work and get a review by experts. This program, which you researched and found to be a major problem for artists is successful and is sponsored by your local museum.

Step 6 - Validate your Credibility

You can ask your mentor for a letter of recommendation that speaks about your leadership in the art therapy club and your involvement with the portfolio review program. This will increase your credibility.

Step 7 - Earn your Target SAT / ACT score

You decide to take the standardized test three times in order to achieve your target score. Then you will spend three months solving problems every day. Your target score of 1560 is achieved on your last attempt.

You get into Yale, NYU and other top schools.

Summary

In step 4 of ACHIEVE, you gained some tools to figure out what you really want to do in life.

You can take aptitude tests, write down all your interests, and find the intersections. Spending even 15 minutes per day exploring your intersections can help clarify your goals. You also learned that online research is not enough to pick a career, and you will have to talk to real professionals in your desired field. In order to do this, you learned the skill of "Online Outreach," which is basically coldemailing professionals you don't know to set up an informational call.

You can refer back to this chapter for the templates to reach out. Action Steps

Online aptitude test

Consider careers that combine your interests

Reach out to 10 professionals in the fields that you are interested in online or through family/friends/counselors

Chapter 10: Step 5 Of Achieve

You've done your research on your interests and the career options available to you. Perhaps you have also spoken to professionals in the field through Zoom. You should have noticed a theme to your interests by now. It's time for you to put it down.

Your application theme

Your why is the underlying reason you want to attend a top university. Your theme is how you want to get there. Imagine climbing a mountain. The Ivy League diploma at the top will unlock opportunities and jobs for you. Your theme is the path you choose. Some are steep and fast while others are windy, long and windy. You will need the right tools to do each task. You should have extra tools and comfortable shoes if your theme is long and windy. You must show others that you can endure the long journey.

My number one mistake is that students don't have an application theme. What is an application theme? You don't need an application theme if you have many extracurriculars that are unrelated.

A theme applicant would organize activities and classes that are related to their interests. I chose classes that would help me prepare for the writing and reading required in law school. I was involved in the local government, participated on the debate team at my community college, and completed a law internship. An admissions officer will review my application and determine what my career path will be.

The theme may also be called a niche or spike. All of these terms echo the idea that if you create a story about yourself and the things you care about, you will be able to stand out among the thousands of students who don't know what they want to do. Think like an artist to stand out.

Would you send one example of your work to an artist who is applying for a creative job? No! To show them the type of art you are capable of creating, you should bring a portfolio.

Think of your college application as an artistic portfolio. You may have seen the passion project. This is where you create your own extracurricular such as a social media platform for mental health awareness. One passion project is not sufficient. There are many students who can start blogs or debate clubs. So how can you make your mark?

Passion portfolios are the secret

Although one project alone, such as a mentorship program for girls interested STEM, might not be sufficient, you can combine multiple projects to show your theme. MIT Dean of Admission Stu Schill stated that portfolios students can submit that show the independent work they have done can enhance applicants' applications.[13]

There are many types of passion portfolio builders. Choose 2-3 to pursue in high school.

7 Passion portfolio builders

1) Internships

Internships allow you to try out a job before you commit to a career.

Internships can be for a short time, lasting only one month. Or they could last years if your boss is impressed with your abilities. You might be interested in becoming a lawyer but you find out that you don't get the time you want. It is also clear that you don't like working in an office. This information will help you get a better job and a better career.

Internships are not only a great way for you to demonstrate your career direction but they also allow you to build your network which will help you make an impact. You might want to intern with a general physician, but you also may be interested in helping the community educate the public about vaccination clinic locations. Your boss will tell you about it and help you connect with her friend at a local medical marketing firm. This friend can help you gain traction on social networks and increase your reach.

Although you might be able apply online for internships, there aren't many opportunities for high school students to get internships. They can help you stand out. Through informational interviews, you can start your own internships. This is how I got my first legal internship at age 14. 2) Research assistant

These roles allow you to collaborate with professors at universities to learn more about their fields. These roles are great for demonstrating your potential as a STEM (science technology, engineering, and math), pre-med student, or future graduate student.

This is a way for you to "test" whether you want to pursue a career in research. After completing a chemistry internship at my local university, I realized that the lab environment was not for me. This was the first time I had ever tested it. Without it, I don't know if I would still be at med school today, dreading every day. You will be happier if you are open to trying out new career paths and experiences.

For research assistant jobs, I recommend looking into the local universities. You might be able to find a summer internship for high school students at your local university. You can still create your own opportunity by cold-emailing professors to request an informational interview. You would learn what you could do to help them in the informational interview. You can help more people if you are willing to help them.

3) Your own organization

It's a great way for you to stand out. You can choose to start a debate club or a mental health awareness group, depending on your chosen theme.

This will help you stand out as it shows your interest in leadership and allows you to find ways to give back. It doesn't matter if you wait for someone to start your organization. You are the boss!

Start by reflecting on why your organization exists, the problems it solves, and how you can help it. You might be shocked at how few women are software engineers. So you create mentorship and conferences to help more women get into software engineering. To make a difference, you decide to use your Monday, Tuesday, and Friday free time to work on this project. 4) Professional organization

You could be a leader in a number of well-established organizations. HOSA is an organization that supports health professions. DECA is available for business. These organizations often have leadership boards at both the national and state levels.

Top students might be elected president of their club chapter. However, it is possible to stand out by applying for national or international positions. One of my students, for example, was able to obtain a position at the PTSA national level. This helped her stand out from the crowd and help her get into Harvard.

Start by researching the professional associations that are available in your area of interest. Look at their websites to see how elections work for both national and international positions. What are your chances of being selected? Zero. However, if you apply, they are greater than zero. 5) Competitions

Many people have asked whether it is necessary to receive awards in order to be admitted into the Ivy League. While not essential, competitions can help admissions officers see where you rank for your chosen theme. Many students apply to major in math. Imagine Sally is a brilliant math student, and Bob is equally talented in math. However, Sally enters a national competition, and wins. Sally is more likely to prove her theme than Bob, even though they might share the same intellectual potential.

National and international competitions are the best to enter to make your mark. You can also stand out by naming and collaborating with notable companies, such as Google or Intel.

Start by looking up the most prestigious competitions within your major or area of interest. Next, check out the eligibility requirements and apply. You have a 100% chance to lose if you don't apply. You might also learn new things about the fields and meet people at the competitions. 6) Selective summer programs

Many summer programs are available, but many do not make you stand out. You can determine if a program is right for you by examining the selection process, which should be below 20%. If the program is competitive and offers full scholarships, it will be a good program.

Summer programs can be a great way for you to discover your career interests and network with other students in the field. These programs can assist you in finding research assistant jobs or meeting other people with the same passions. This can help you to think of a new organization and build your passion portfolio.

The Research Science Institute (RSI), a summer program that's free, gives you the chance to work with scientists from MIT.

7) Sports

Sport is a great way for you to stand out. Your dream school may have an athletic department that is looking for you, regardless of whether you are a soccer player or a cross-country runner. You should research which colleges offer the sport at the varsity level if you are interested in continuing your chosen sport in college.

It's important to know the rules of the National Collegiate Athletic Association (NCAA), as this is the non-profit that regulates student athletes.

[14] Register with the NCAA to be eligible and review the instructions for contacting the coaches at your dream schools to get started. [15] Harvard's athletic website states, "To contact the respective head coach who will send you a questionnaire or direct to Harvard's online recruitment forms."

For coaches to chat with you, there are specific NCAA rules. In some sports, coaches cannot reach you until your junior year. [16] I spoke with a Harvard-recruited athlete who said that it was important to show interest in the school . Coaches can only recommend a few athletes for admissions. They will choose the most likely applicants if they accept. How would you feel if your neck was pulled for a student only to find out that they chose another school?

Brainstorm your passion portfolio builders

It's now time to think about possible projects that could help you determine if this career is right for you. Your passion project should combine your interests (e.g., pharmaceutical law) and help you network with others in the industry or try it yourself. YouTube is great, but until you experience it for yourself, you will not know what it is like to work in a law office or any other place.

As a Reporter, I would recommend that you start your project. This will allow you to research the industry online and talk to people who are in the field. It is possible to make an impact by sharing your knowledge with other students and helping them understand the possibilities for a career in this field. You could start a blog, YouTube channel or podcast to share useful information with students. These projects can be linked to fundraising for a particular cause or to help you and your friends obtain internships.

It is important to remember that "reporter" does not mean that you are an expert. You learn alongside your audience and ask real experts how they got there. This a simple way to approach your project. If you are passionate about the topic, this will make you feel less like an outsider.

This step is crucial. It's important to experiment with different things to find what works for you. Learning from any experience is a sure way to win. If you decide you don't want to go to a particular intersection, you can always return to other intersections and pick another one.

This next step will allow you to brainstorm passion projects that will make you stand out. Here are some questions that will help you organize your thoughts:

What projects relate to your future career goal or can help you develop the skills for your career goal? What projects help your

community or school?

What are the projects that excite you more than Netflix on Friday nights?

What projects sound impressive? Will it make people say, "Wow, how do you do that?"

What projects push you outside your comfort zone?

Pick the project to start

After you have compiled a list of ideas, ask these questions to narrow down your choices. Idealerweise, you'd answer yes to most or all of these questions.

Is this project related to your career goals or helps you build the skills necessary for that career? Colleges are interested in seeing that you have a clear direction for your career. This shows that you have learned about yourself and that you are mature.

Is this project going to help your school or community? Admissions officers are not only looking for students who excel academically. They also look for students who are willing to give back to the college, take part in seminars, be kind and helpful to their roommates. College is as social as it is intellectual.

Is this project exciting to you? Would you choose it over Netflix on Friday nights?

Picking a project that excites you will help you stay motivated towork on it. This will probably happen after hours of honors or AP homework on weekdays. Therefore, ensure your project passes Friday Night Netflix Test.

Is the project impressive? Cal Newport, in How to Be a High School Superstar explains how "accomplishments which are difficult to explain are better" than those that are easy to do. For example, it is more difficult to explain starting a high school band than becoming a best-selling author. This is a good indicator that people will be impressed by your accomplishments.

A good slogan or a simple sentence can explain impressive projects. This is why you need to think about the end result of your project. My Harvard classmate invented a "one minute mobile charger." Another example would be writing a best-selling textbook in your field. Your project will be more memorable if it is more witty.

Is this project pushing you beyond your comfort zone, making you feel uncomfortable? Top schools want to see you pushing yourself academically and personally. This means challenging yourself and taking on new challenges. You can foster creativity and learn which activities you love, and discover the incredible things you can do.

Ask your counselors, teachers, and other mentors for help in choosing the right one. You should choose the project that excites you most and aligns with your career goals.

I was interested in medical law and pursued internships that were law/medical. In order to improve my public speaking skills, I joined the debate team at my local community college. Later, I would help others overcome their fear of public speaking by starting a debate team at my high school. It is important to find activities that are related to your passion portfolio.

Skill: Finding your theme

Your theme is all about your passions, skills, and problems.

(Passions + Skills + Issues) = Theme

One of my students is passionately involved in STEM and skilled in networking. She also hates the lack of women in STEM. She followed the theme formula and discovered her theme. Then she created mentoring groups to help more girls get into STEM fields.

Reflect on these questions to help you decide your application theme. Ask yourself these questions to discover your passions: What topics do you enjoy discussing (e.g., anime or climate change)? What are your interests in particular fields or careers?

To discover your strengths: What skills have you acquired from past classes, clubs, and academic programs? Which topics are you most interested in hearing from others?

These questions will help you identify your problem. What are your most difficult problems?

One of my students is passionately interested in robotics and AI, and proficient at coding. His focus is on teaching the next generation technology use in a productive manner and introducing them to technology careers.

High school was my theme. I wanted to help high school students understand current events and learn communication skills through the debate group I started.

It doesn't matter what theme you choose, it will be easier to find a project to begin with!

ACHIEVE in action - Law example

Imagine you dream of becoming a lawyer. Since your aunt was a lawyer and introduced you to the profession, you have been fascinated by it. It's all there: watching Law & Order, doing mock trials and learning about the latest Supreme Court cases.

You should know that there are many people who want to become lawyers. They apply to top schools such as Harvard. So make sure you have the right tools to stand out with the ACHIEVE program.

Step 1 - Aim for As in Advanced Classes

You'll see that the steps are arranged in a way that makes sense. Step 2 - Conduct an Activity Audit

There aren't many activities you can cut. You're good at doing what you love and it contributes to your career goals.

Step 3 - Help your Teacher Help You

Step three is a great way to build a stronger relationship with your teachers. You have a special relationship with your history teacher and decide to meet up at his office to get to know him better. Your history teacher realizes that visual content is vital for engaging students in history classes. He would love more videos and skits.

You create a proposal to recruit drama students to perform some of the most important events from history. You also make a decision to recruit the film department. This is a department that mainly films athletic events but might be interested in this. Your teacher is thrilled and contacts the head of the drama department as well as the film department to get you started.

You have established a strong relationship with your history teacher, and you are ready to start this project.

Step 4 - Ignite your Interests

You are certain that you want to become a lawyer. So you contact local

judges and lawyers for informational interviews.

You learn about a volunteer opportunity at youth court through your

interviews. You develop great relationships with the program director as well

as the judge by attending this court every week. A judge will connect you with a former classmate from law school to discuss your interest in a legal

internship.

Step 5 - Execute your Theme

You are available to help this lawyer organize and file his documents. Gradually, you take on more responsibility. You may be asked to assist in taking notes during expert interviews. You can also be taken along to court cases, so you can see how the jury is selected.

Step 6 - Validate your Credibility

Once you feel that your internship is going well, you can start to build your credibility by writing articles for local publications about your experience. Although it may take a while to see what type of articles are popular, one article will eventually be published in a major law publication. Your mentor in law will gladly submit a letter. She has greatly appreciated your organization and optimism.

Step 7- Earn your Target SAT / ACT score

You're a natural test-taker so the SAT will not be a problem for you. You get admitted to Dartmouth and Harvard!

Summary

In step 5 of ACHIEVE, you learned the difference between your "why" and your "theme."

You also learned about the 7 types of Passion Portfolio builders, which can help you discover your unique way of standing out. Then you learned how to find your theme by combining your passion, skills, and a cause you care about.

Finally, you can reflect on a series of questions that will help you brainstorm what type of project you should do and how to make sure that it is impactful, challenging, and related to your future goals.

Action Steps

Define your application theme

Determine the types of projects that you are interested in. Then, narrow down to one project.

Chapter 11: Step 6 Of Achieve - Validate Your Credibility

"Youth making an impact." "Driven by medicine--and the law." These were my headlines in the articles about me that appeared in local newspapers. To show that I was a leader within my community, I included them when I applied to colleges. This helped me stand out from other students in my area and secured a place in the Ivy League.

You are competing with top students who have amazing extracurriculars when you apply to the Ivy League. How can you stand out from the crowd with your passion portfolio? It's crucial to prove your credibility. You can validate your credibility in many ways, including being published, winning awards and building a large following.

I spoke to one Ivy League student who said that submitting his piano recording had proven his talent more than the many piano awards he has won. The admission committee was able to trust his abilities and accept him.

While anyone can claim to be a world-class pianist without any proof, few people will believe them.

Increasing your impact

Your ability to make an impact in your local community is proof of how you can contribute to the college community. You might help spread the word about vaccine clinics or get 100 people to sign-up. It's great to start a project, but it's better to make a difference.

After you get your project started, think about ways you can make it more impactful. What about partnering with clubs from other schools? Could you blog about your learnings and help others?

There are many ways to increase the impact of your project, depending on your goals. You might not get published in Science magazine if you're on a science track. However, you can show your interest in a career and land internships by expressing your curiosity to mentors. An internship can help you build your reputation and increase the impact of your project, especially if it is with well-respected companies. Other ways to increase your impact are to be able to raise money or involve more people.

Admission officers want to see evidence that you are trying your best for your community. Perhaps you're selling candy bars door-to-door to help raise funds for your church.

Imagine if your friends get involved or you start posting on social networks. Schools across the country will love your ideas and want to help. Social media has many benefits. It can open up a lot of possibilities, and even help you build your team to make your ideas more impactful. You can take on leadership roles and coordinate fundraising events that reach thousands of children. Although it may seem daunting at first, the hardest part of any fundraising project is the beginning. Increasing its impact will come easier as time passes.

You have many options to increase your impact. You could present your research results at a conference if you're a student at a local college. Send your work in to be published. Perhaps you can help other students get a position in research?

Using Social Media

Social media is a powerful tool for building an audience and raising awareness about your issue. Imagine you have started a debate group and want to increase your reach by using other communication tools. Social media can be used to reach people around the globe and to teach public speaking skills. You can use YouTube, Instagram TikTok or Twitter to share your expertise and experience, which will be evidence of your impact on your community and beyond.

If you use social media and have a large enough following, it may be easier to reach influencers in your industry. Influencers are always looking to increase their reach. You can help them by sharing their book, research, or "whatever" with your audience.

Media attention

Attach any media attention that you receive to your college application. Published articles/features about you, whether in a local newspaper, or on a well-known blog, will show colleges that you are creative and dedicated. Sometimes, newspapers will reach out to you to ask if they can write about you. Two local newspapers featured me in high school for my community work, which included a seminar on job training for teens.

A few newspapers have sections that feature teens or a community profile. Get in touch with the editor of that section to find out if you are a good fit. Journalists are always on the lookout for the next great story!

You can also pursue them if they don't reach you. Establish relationships with journalists in your local area and in your field. Try to get to know them. You can start by reading their work, and then send them questions and encouraging comments. You can then send them a pitch for being featured in their section.

PR Pitches

Then, you can pitch an idea to them of what their readers would enjoy. Make sure you do your research to ensure that your work is relevant to the writer's area of interest. Darrell Etherington, TechCrunch's Science editor, uses Twitter to solicit pitches.

An example pitch:

Hi [Name],

Your work has been a constant source of inspiration for me over the

past year.

Your recent post on "Topic" really resonated with my and reminded of the project that I'm currently working on, [impact and benefits from your project].

It is available here: [insert blog link for more information]. This is what I would love for you to share with your audience. We are grateful for your insight and tips on the [industry] industry.

Best wishes

[Your Name]

To get your story published, you'll likely need to pitch multiple journalists. If you're consistent and build these relationships, you may not only get a published article with your name on it, but also become a mentor. You should save any article that is published so that you can add it to your college application.

It is important to be able to communicate your value and what you bring to the table when pitching yourself. Writing your resume is a great way to do this. Your school activities can be included in your resume instead of your work experience.

Skill: resume writing for impact

My mom used to tell me that the tallest grass blade gets cut down, as a way of keeping me humble. Although it sounds like a deep Chinese proverb, in actuality, it's an outdated concept in today's fast-paced and mobile world.

My first job was after college. I brought a list of all my achievements to my annual performance review. Even though I met with him on a weekly basis, he knew what projects I was working on and was amazed at how much I accomplished. It's unlikely that anyone will notice your successes and value if you don't share them. This is also true for college applications. Your admissions officer may not appreciate your outstanding contributions if you're too modest about your achievements.

Imagine, for example, that you were a translator in your school's soccer team. You might write in your resume or the activities section of an application that you "translated for the tournament soccer team." But would this help a reader to understand why you were so important?

This might be a problem for admissions officers who may not find it impressive because they haven't been very specific about what you did.

This is the real story of a translator who applied for Olympic teams, but didn't mention it in their application. If you have ever been to a country where the language is not your native tongue, you will understand how crucial it is to have a guide who can help you navigate the country and avoid making mistakes. Although this student was able to keep his team healthy and help them find all they needed at the highest level of the game's play, it almost cost him his admission. One of his letters of recommendations mentioned his international influence and his high level of professionalism in translations.

After spending thousands on career coaching, I have learned these tips and can't wait share them with my readers. This formula will help you write bullets for your resume and demonstrate your impact: result + action.

Let's say, for example, you partner with local schools to hold an auction. Now, how do we spice this description up? The result is the most important. Include the number of schools that participated. This effort is impressive. Give numbers and details.

"Raised 13,550 USD for Habitat For Humanity through coordinating an auction featuring three schools." You could keep adding details but you should talk about the impact immediately and then detail the actions you took.

Ask yourself "So what?" to find the impact or result. In the previous example, you have partnered with three high school students to host an auction fundraiser.

You might think, "Cool, but what?" But the truth is, it helped Habitat for Humanity raise 10,000 dollars. BINGO! This is the end result!

These are just a few more examples:

Raised 10,000 dollars for Habitat for humanity by partnering with three high schools to organize an auction fundraiser.

Helped 27 students prioritize mental wellbeing through

organization of 5 mental wellness workshops and 45+ motivational posts on social media

Connected 17 high school females to leading tech experts by creating a mentorship program to inspire more females to go into STEM

ACHIEVE in action - Math example

Let's say you love math. Since you were little, multiplication was a favorite subject.

Step 1 - Aim for As in Advanced Classes

You are placed in the most advanced math track at school so that you can take AP Calculus B/C your senior year. To stretch yourself, you may even take a theoretical algebra class in your junior year. Despite feeling confident in math, your mind isn't clear on how to stand out. The Ivies have many students who score excellent on the math section.

Start at step 1 and work your way up to AP English. To make sure that you are on the right path, you will review drafts of your essays together with your teacher.

Step 2 - Conduct an Activity Audit

Next, you can move on to step 2. Then you move to step 2. You decide

to stop being in chess, photography, or community service clubs.

Step 3 - Help your Teacher Help You

You decide to give your extra time to your math teacher. Ask your friends what their biggest problems are with math learning. The one thing they discover is that many students don't want to learn it because it doesn't make sense in real life. They would prefer it to be less theoretical and more concrete. Your teacher will help you to use real-world examples such as how P values are used in marketing to determine which advertisements perform better.

Step 4 - Ignite your Interests

You have built a relationship with your teacher, and you are now ready to start your theme search. You search for careers that appeal to math enthusiasts and come across data science. You research the job market to find promising trends. You find an online conference in data science that you want to register for. You must email your teachers to let them know that the conference will take place during school. Your math teacher is thrilled to hear that they all said yes!

Even though you don't understand many of their words, the conference taught you so much. Send an email to the speaker you most like and ask for a quick phone call. You follow up with an email if she doesn't reply.

Surprised to discover that she replied with some times she is available the next day.

You can chat with her and ask some very well-researched queries. She is impressed! After the call, you send a thank-you note to her and ask for a job shadowing opportunity. You are grateful to her for helping you, and the job shadowing opportunity becomes an internship.

Step 5 - Execute your Theme

Your math teacher receives a letter from a prestigious math program. She immediately thinks about you. You are nominated and receive a glowing letter of support.

You realize the lack of representation in data science during your internship. You care about this issue so you set up a panel to educate more students from your local community about data science. To increase attendance, you reach out to campus cultural clubs.

Students email you asking when they can attend the next event after your event was a great success. You form a club for data science that organizes talks and conferences to promote this career.

Step 6 - Validate your credibility

Contact your local newspaper to find out if they are available. You have completed your junior year and are ready to take the SATs. You are an outstanding applicant when you apply for college. Your data science topic is strong and includes activities. Your teachers and mentor in data science write impressive letters of recommendation. Finally, you submit a newspaper article on the conference and its impact.

Step 7- Earn your Target SAT / ACT score

Both practice tests are taken and you score significantly higher on the

ACT. You study for two months to reach your target score of 35/36. You can get into Princeton, MIT, and many other top schools!

Summary

In step 6 of ACHIEVE, you learned that your passion portfolio is going to be judged by admissions officers based on the level of passion and impact that you display.

This chapter gave you some tips for increasing the impact of your project, such as by using social media and pitching your project to local/online publications.

Finally, you learned how to rewrite your resume or profile bullet points with result + action to make sure the reader understands the impact that you've achieved.

Action Steps

Think of 3 ways you can increase your influence and boost your credibility.

Pitch 5 magazines or publications in your area that are related to your project

Write your bulletins using result + action to keep track of your achievements each semester.

1. Get Exceptional Grades

Quite simply, you need have exceptional grades, not just good grades. You need to be in the top 10% of your class and preferably in the top 1%-5%. That's the reality. If your grades and class rank aren't in this elite range, you don't have much of a chance of being accepted. Grades are the first sign of proof that you are a capable student. You must have fantastic grades throughout high school, every grade, every year.

Remember, everyone that applies to ivy league colleges have to have fantastic grades. That's the first "must." To be seriously considered for acceptance this is the first hurdle you must jump over.

2. Take The Most Rigorous Courses and Schedule That Your School Offers

If you don't, chances are someone else in your grade has. I'm specifically talking about Advanced Placement and Honors Level Classes. If your school offers these levels, it is expected that you take the classes and earn spectacular grades. Ivy League colleges need to see that you challenged yourself consistently and were able to perform at an extremely high level. It's not enough to have great grades, you have to earn those grades in the most challenging classes offered.

It should also go without saying, but you must take core-classes every year of high school. For example, even though your high school may not require you to take a science class or math class senior year, you will be at a huge disadvantage if you don't when it comes time to applying.

Your transcript will be closely scrutinized and checked and double-checked to make sure you have challenged yourself in every possible way. Don't give their admissions committee any reason to punish you, take the most demanding course-load you can from start to finish.

3. Score Exceptionally Well On Standardized Tests

Ivy league colleges require you to take either the SAT/ACT and SAT Subject Tests (also referred to as SAT II's). You must score in the top percentile nationally to have a realistic chance of admission. The competition is too fierce out there to not have elite test scores. True, test scores aren't everything but it is a key component of your profile that must match your grades. If you have fantastic grades and average test scores, the colleges will want to know why? And, you better have a great explanation of why that is or you simply won't be getting in. Sorry to be harsh, but that's the reality of the process. At the highest level, ivy league colleges aren't looking for excuses, they want to see evidence of your ability.

My advice is to start early in your junior year of high school taking standardized tests. This way it will give you the time you may need to re-take the tests at a later date. It's also a good idea to take both the SAT and the ACT. You will then get to choose the one you've scored better on to send to your colleges. The lower score will not be sent and become your little secret.

SAT II's are also a factor in admissions. Most Ivy League colleges will want you to submit at least two subject tests. I would recommend you take at least three and if the scores aren't sufficient, you the can re-take the tests or choose to take the test in different subjects to hopefully improve your scores.

SAT II's vs. ACT With Writing. Some ivy league colleges will offer you to submit the ACT with writing test in lieu of SAT II's (subject tests). That is a good option for someone that feels more comfortable taking the ACT test rather than zeroing in on two subjects.

Good advice would be to take all the test, SAT, SAT II's, and the ACT with Writing and then form a plan of submitting your highest scores to the colleges. You really don't have anything to lose, as the colleges will only see the scores you send in.

4. Know Yourself

Really think about what separates you from everyone else? Realize what it is that makes you different from others and what makes you special. I'm talking beyond the classroom and school. Here are some questions to think about:

How has your upbringing impacted you as a person?

Do you have a story to share that shows hardship or perserverance?

What areas and subjects are you interested in and why?

How have you succeeded and why has it been important for you to do so?

What would attending an Ivy League College mean to your future?

How does your community or neighborhood view you?

Explain your family dynamic?

What responsibilities besides school do you have?

Why have you taken part in the activities that you have?

5. Do You Have a Unique Talent or Ability?

Are you exceptional at something that we should know about? Athletics is an obvious one, but what about musically, theatrically, or educationally? What is your unique talent or ability that makes you standout from your peers and that you have demonstrated a high level of success in?

If you don't have an answer or a specific response to the above question, that's okay. But, be warned colleges will ask. They want to see proof of your special skill-set that they can add to their student-body. It's a time for you to be recognized for you talents and don't be shy about promoting yourself. They are looking for something besides great grades and test scores to admit you. If you have a proven ability, please let it be known!

Throughout the college application process is your time to get notices. It's the culmination of all of your hard-work throughout the years. Please realize that it's okay to self-promote and boast a bit, college admissions officers want to learn as much as they can before they make their decision. Try to make their job easier than it is, show them all that you are and capable of. It will help and hopefully pay off for you in the end.

6. Have You Had An Academic Experience That Sets You Apart?

Have you taken college courses? How about participated in a summer program on a college campus that was academic specific? Have you applied for and been selected to take part in an advanced academic program during your high school years?

Believe it or not, there are a ton of ways for you to take your learning to the next level while in high school. College's know this, because every college offers these types of programs. Ideally, during your high school years, you've searched for the best academic programs, applied to, and been accepted into them. It really separates you from many of your peers and will show the colleges how serous you are as a student.

Academic programs are a great way to continue your education during the summer months or during the school year or even during school vacation weeks. If you have done these types of programs, please let the college know. Show them all the hard work you've done and your accomplishments. Make note of any awards or achievements that you were selected for and include what you learned at each stop. It's important.

7. Are You A Community Star?

Are you a star in your community? Maybe you live in a really small town and have been anointed the next big thing? Or, you could live in a big city and have been able to standout and make a difference on a large scale? Include your story and how you've been an impact on the people of your community. Beyond the typically community service hours that many high schools require, what have you done on your own to impact the people of your community in a positive way?

Remember, it's not just about you and your talents, it's what you choose to do with them! Are you a leader that has worked tirelessly making a change in your town or city? Let's see the proof and evidence of your actions and explain why you have chosen to do what you did.

It takes a special person to stand up and make a change, if that's you, you are doing great things that should be recognized. Have you been featured in the local newspaper, or been interviewed on television, how about publically acknowledged for your actions? Now is the time for that recognition to be sent to your colleges, so they can learn too.

8. Get The Best Teacher Recommendations That You Can!

Most ivy league colleges will require at least two teacher recommendations. Your job is to make sure whichever two teachers are writing yours, write the best one's they've ever written. By nature, the teacher recommendation tends to address you academically. That's fine, but if you are a college admissions person, there's only so many times that you can read about what a great student John Smith has been. Tell your teachers to explain why you are such a good student with examples, stories, and personal narratives to ram home the point. We get it, you're a good student, but what type of person are you in the classroom? How do you impact the learning of others in your classes? Are you a leader when you do group work and go above the minimum requirements?

Remember, college applications readers want to read an interesting story, not the same old story. Make sure that you are able to work with the teacher writing your college recommendation to tell the story that you want to be told. It's important. From my experience, teachers would welcome such a request. They want to sit down with you individually and talk about what makes you a special student and person. Remember, this is your time to shine, make sure that your teacher recommendation is shining brightly on you.

9. Guidance Counselor Recommendation

Your guidance counselor recommendation is also a requirement at ivy league colleges. You want this recommendation to show another side of you, besides your abilities as a student. Remember, the teachers will write on that topic, the guidance counselor ideally will be able to tie in everything remarkable about you in a way that demonstrates their personal relationship with you and your family. Have your guidance counselor really think about what makes you special and tell the story for the college to see.

It's important that whatever is submitted is up to your standards. Guidance Counselors often have many recommendations to do for other students, but if you are applying to an ivy league college, you need yours to stand out. Work with them to understand the approach that you want to take and even incorporate some examples that you think is important for them to write about. Hey, it's your recommendation that they're writing, why not have some input on it?

Guidance Counselors really have the ability to think outside the box when it comes time to writing their recs. They could choose to write about a variety of topics both in and outside of school, delivering a powerful message. The relationship that you have with your guidance counselor is an important one, so don't wait until the Fall of your senior year in getting to know them. They are on your side and there is no more meaningful time when they are writing your recommendation for that relationship to be expressed.

10. Alumni Recommendation & Other Recommenders

My advice is to look for an alumni of the college you are applying to and work with them to write a recommendation on your behalf. This may take some time and effort, but can very much be worth it. Colleges always want to hear from their alumni, especially from ones if they are active in their role. Obtaining an alumni recommendation is welcomed, whether the colleges want to admit it or not. They will get to see someone that has great familiarity with the college and read their reasons for writing you a recommendation. That's powerful.

Making a connection with an alumni can be a hard task. You will have to do your best to network and ask as many people as you know if they can put you in touch with their connection. Once established, you then will have to form a relationship with that person in hopes for them to write something spectacular on your behalf. Sometimes you are one person away, other times it can be really hard to locate a person fitting your need. My advice is to search for alumni as best as you can, they'll appreciate the effort and ideally be on your side during this process. If they can help, they will gladly offer their assistance and that's all you can ask for.

A quick note on other recommenders; these people can be community leaders, a boss, a program leader, or anyone else you see fit in writing a glowing recommendation. You don't think a college would be impressed if you had your local mayor or police chief write a recommendation? They sure will. It's always great to show another perspective from someone of influence. It makes you stand-out even more than you already do and also makes you seem more personable, because with each letter they are learning more about you, and that's the goal!

11. Apply to Attend a Program or Opportunity at a Specific College

Did you know that colleges offer a variety of programs specifically intended for high school students? Many colleges target specific groups of students (STEM Programs, minority students, first generation college students). Please take advantage of these offerings and research the best fit for yourself.

Many programs have strict applications and deadlines that you need to be aware in order to successfully apply. Colleges will work with you greatly to see your intent in their specific school and often times refer you to the most appropriate program or event.

Colleges also hold specialized visitation days and events throughout the school year. It's not too early to begin looking to attend these events in your sophomore year. It's a great way to introduce yourself to a prospective college and vice versa. Many admission representatives will appreciate your eagerness to begin the process and immediately put you on their radar moving forward.

12. Interview

Even though the trend is for colleges not to require interviews these days, there are still many great ways for you to take advantage of the interviewing process. Ivy League Colleges will allow you to self-schedule an interview on their campus with an admissions representative. This is a great way to learn more about the college as well as give yourself an opportunity to impress.

One recent move that many ivy league schools have been doing is allowing alumni interviews. This interview would be conducted in convenience with the applicants home area at a mutually agreed location. These interviews are given by alumni who have varied backgrounds and experiences, but all have attended the ivy league school of your dreams. They have influence with their admissions committee and their input is encouraged. I've had students meet for their interview at their local coffee shop and I've had students interview in the office of an alumni at their place of business.

Interviews are just another way for you to standout and become noticed for your achievements. This is a must for any ivy league applicant. If you live in a metropolitan area, the ease of an alumni interview getting scheduled is a plus. If you live in a more isolated area, this process may be a bit more challenging but surely can still be arrange.

13. Attend College Information Sessions at your School and Community

College information sessions at your high school are a great way to get familiar with the college representative, who may be your actual admissions reader. I've heard many of times from admissions representatives who have visited our school and been impressed with an introduction or question a student had. Admissions reps are people too and like to be treated well. If you can make an impression on them, they will certainly remember you when it comes time to read your application materials.

The odds of a big crowd attending an ivy league college's information session at your school is rare and gives you even more of incentive of attending. The rep will speak about their college in detail and answer any questions that you may have. It's a wonderful way in an informal setting to connect with your admissions rep.

Another wonderful way to get noticed is to attend events and visits to your local city or area. Many times college admission reps will hold events at night or on a weekend in an area where many students will apply from. You and your parents are encouraged to attend such an even and learn as much as you can from the presentation and from the admissions officer. Many representatives will offer further communication from themselves, a sign they are willing to become personable throughout the process.

14. Network Behind The Scenes

One of your goals when applying to an ivy league college is to learn as much as you can about that particular college. Some ways for you to do this is to ask any adult you know if they can connect with an alumni from the college you are interested in. I've found that alumni are more than willing to talk about their college years and experience. It gives them a way to go back in time and boast about their college-years, often the best time in one's life. Your parents, boss, program director, or even your teachers are a great place to begin asking for these connections.

With the presence of social media these days, it shouldn't be too difficult for you to track down an alumni. Once you do, have a few specific questions that you want to ask as well as their advice in the application process. They will have great insights on what worked and what did not. Don't be too invasive and aggressive, rather listen and make note of their suggestions.

Another great piece of advice is to ask your guidance counselor for an introduction to any former student that attends your dream ivy league school. These introductions are rather easy and you can quickly email, text, or connect through social media. Recent former students are a great resource to have at your disposal, they can add great value throughout the process and be able to answer any question that you may have.

15. Learn the Difference of Each Ivy League College

Learn the differences that each ivy league college has from each other, from the basics of location and student population, to the advanced of different majors and study-abroad opportunities. The differences really make up what separates them from each other. We know they are all great schools and offer a variety of programs and supports that are second to none. What we don't know, is what specifically speaks to you, the applicant. Are you looking for a specific athletic club team that you want to participate in, or are you looking for a college that's on a trimester schedule? Are you looking for a researched based focus of study or do you prefer a more of a liberal arts education? The questions can go on and on, but you are the only one that can provide the answers.

The more you learn about the ivy league colleges, the more you will become familiar with them. When you combine that knowledge with meeting admissions representatives and visiting college campuses, you will get a great feel on where you want to spend the next four years of your life. This is a major step for any young person and a huge commitment to take, please do your due diligence during the process because at the end of the day, you are the one that is going to have to make the decision.

College is a great opportunity that will provide you with an amazing experience, please enjoy the process of applying to college as well. Even though it's stressful and contains many moving parts, try to take a step back and appreciate all of your hard work that you have done to get to this point!

16. Write A Great College Essay

You have so many options when it comes to writing your college essay. There are many prompts that you can choose from, so choose wisely. This is your opportunity to really show yourself and tell your story. The college essay must be well-written, proof read, and edited properly. Please make sure you have a well trusted editor available to you when needed and can offer you a different perspective than your own.

There are many books and articles written on how to craft a great college essay, my advice is to show the reader something that you feel comfortable with and delivering a powerful message. It's a great opportunity that you have to show the readers another facet of yourself, while impressing them with your style and delivery.

Don't overthink the process. Choose which essay prompt you would like to address and dive in. Write what comes to mind and go with it. Your editor will be able to give good feedback, then you can revise it until you feel comfortable. Like previously mentioned, as long as the essay is proofread and edited well, your message will come across as you intended.

17. Indicating Your College Major

This is a step that many don't understand how important it really is. When you indicate a college major on your application, that shows the college what academic field you are interested in. As you may have heard, some college majors are more difficult getting accepted into than others. Take that information under consideration. If you are indicating interest in a very competitive major, you have to be the best of the best of applicants. If there is any doubt in the mind's of the admission committee, that's not a good sign for acceptance. For example, if you are listing your intended major as business, yet your math grades and test scores aren't in the elite range, you may have a problem convincing the admissions committee that you are a worthy candidate.

When in doubt, select undeclared. The reason for this is to not subject yourself to the heavy scrutiny of a specific major and it gives you a bigger pool of applicants to be considered from. When you choose an selected major, let the scrutiny began. Not only will you be looked at by the admissions committee, you will then be passed along to the specific college that your major falls under.

A major is a big choice and decision that you will make someday. Don't overthink this aspect of your application now and let it alter your path. College students typically change their major at least once, close to 70%. Why declare it before you even step on campus? Unless you are 100% on your decision, than go for it, if not, I'd advise otherwise. Please think about it carefully, before you commit.

18. Strongly Consider Applying Early Decision or Restrictive Early Action

I highly recommend you apply early decision or restrictive early action. First let me explain the differences. Many ivy league colleges still have the option to apply Early Decision. This means that you are committed and in agreement that if you select to apply early decision and get accepted you must attend that particular college. Your parents, guidance counselor, and you have to all sign off on the early decision agreement and its details.

The new trend in ivy league college admissions is the Restrictive Early Action Admission. This means that you can only apply to one specific college Restrictive Early, but you can apply to a state college or university early as well. However, if you get accepted into the college you apply restrictive to, you must attend. This is much like Early Decision, just different wording and a bit more flexibility.

If you don't get accepted under either application process, you are free to apply to any other college you would like. Applying "Early" is a great way to show the college how serious you are in attending their school. Obviously if the decision is mutual, you will get accepted and be complete with the college application process earlier, often times in mid-December.

Applying early also gives you a better chance to get accepted, in my opinion. If you've done everything previously outlined in this book, and you then decided to apply early, your advantage gains great momentum to your favor. When you commit to a big decision such as early decision, it makes the job of the admission committee that much easier.

19. Submit All Materials On Time

Please, please, please make sure that you are aware of all deadlines and important dates. Colleges won't wait for anything when they have clearly set deadlines already established. Your materials include: your application and fee, your high school transcript and profile, teacher recommendations, and standardized test scores. No matter how your high school sends their materials in, you must make sure the college gets it in a timely manner. When sending standardized test scores such as the SAT and ACT, please be advised that it often takes weeks when you place your order for the two companies to actually send your scores. This information cannot be lost upon you, and certainly shouldn't be a hold-up for the college in making a decision on your application.

Don't wait until the last minute to check to see if all of your materials are sent in. Please have an open dialogue with your guidance counselor and the teachers that are writing your recommendation. You will then get to make sure that everything is received on time and recorded as such. Don't let anything stand in your way of getting accepted, remember you are trying to impress and come across as a prepared young person, not someone that is missing materials or irresponsible.

20. Complete All Financial Aid Materials Accurately and Timely

When you apply to ivy league colleges, you will be required to complete the CSS Profile (operated by the college board). Please understand the requirements of completing the CSS Profile and all forms that accompany it. You will need your families income reports to fill out the CSS Profile. Colleges have strict deadlines regarding completion of the CSS, be advised.

www.ingramcontent.com/pod-product-compliance
Lightning Source LLC
Chambersburg PA
CBHW050404120526
44590CB00015B/1817